The
Joy
of the Only
Child

The Joy of the Only Child

ELLEN PECK

DELACORTE PRESS / NEW YORK

Grateful acknowledgment is made for permission to use the following material:

Excerpts from *Families: A Memoir and a Celebration* by Wyatt Cooper: Copyright © 1975 by Wyatt Cooper. Used by permission of Harper & Row, Publishers, Inc., and Bantam Books, Inc.

Excerpt from *Yes, I Can* by Sammy Davis, Jr.: Reprinted with the permission of Farrar, Straus & Giroux, Inc., from *Yes, I Can* Copyright © 1965 by Sammy Davis, Jr., Jane Boyar, and Burt Boyar.

Diagrams from *The Mirages of Marriage* by William J. Lederer and Don D. Jackson, M.D.: Reprinted by permission of W. W. Norton & Company, Inc. Copyright © 1968 by W. W. Norton & Company, Inc.

Excerpts from *The Birth Order Factor* by Lucille K. Forer: Copyright © 1976 by Lucille K. Forer with Henry Still. Published by David McKay Company, Inc. Reprinted by permission of the publisher.

Excerpt from *Fear of Flying* by Erica Jong: Copyright © 1973 by Erica Mann Jong. Reprinted by permission of Holt, Rinehart and Winston, Publishers.

Manufactured in the United States of America
First printing

Library of Congress Cataloging in Publication Data

Peck, Ellen, 1942–
   The joy of the only child.

   Includes index.
   1. Only child.   I. Title.
HQ777.3.P4   301.42'7   77-2359
ISBN 0-440-04262-3

ACKNOWLEDGMENTS

To Ruth Hunt, Ph.D., and Heidi Toffler (two very special only children) I owe thanks for several priceless hours of insightful dialogue.

For sharing a wealth of professional experience and viewpoints, thanks to:

Dr. E. James Lieberman
Alvin Toffler
Julie A. Cleare
Dr. Teresa Marciano
Dr. Jessie Bernard
Shirley Radl
Leona Train Rienow
C. Ray Fowler
Dr. David Martin

William J. Lederer
Joyce Halstedt
Rebecca Liswood, Ph.D.
Herbert Robbins, Ph.D.
Dr. Charles Arnold
Sylvia Wassertheil-Smoller
Marcielle Lakos
Delores Ann Hudson

For essential information:
Cynthia Green, Celia Miller, Susan Lowe of Zero Population Growth
Greg Duncan of the Institute for Social Research
Donald Mann of Negative Population Growth
Gail McKirdy of the National Organization for Non-Parents
Vera Patchek of the Population Reference Bureau
Hank Curtis of the Wilderness Society
Ed Passerini of the University of Alabama
Dr. Fred Allman of the Sports Medicine Clinic

For the arduous task of attempting to research countless birth orders by various and imaginative methods and against overwhelming odds, thanks forever to the Good Samaritan members of what came to be called "The Blue Card Club":

Debbi Morgan
Donna Wurzbach
Frederick Kavanagh
Arline Newton
James P. O'Callaghan
Jim Chamberlin
Ralph Cohen
Charlotte Stiefel
Connie Matthews

Meredith Hickson
Linda Barnett
Irwin Auerbach
Karen Lange
Lynn Page
Lynn Marks
Susan Gufert
Nancy Bedell
Marcy Wenzler

Anne Bingham
Mary Hillesland
Robin Faber
Lisa Dellinger
Vernon and Susan Sanders
Ann and M.S. Hollyfield
Joyce Carlson
Florence Boulanger
Adeline Rosemire
Susan Wetterau

For "telling it like it is" in lengthy letters, hundreds should be thanked, in particular Lynn Hill, Susan Neisuler, Patricia Krauska, Sue Todd Yates, Carol Bok, Mary Kay Osborn, Kitty Rea, Marjorie Robbins, Janice Hall Bottenus, Corky Ettinger.

Acknowledgments

For help along the way that often included sustaining encouragement: Joyce Snyder, Dr. Louise Tyrer, Joyce Raffaelle, Ann Phillips, Lydia Vuynovich, Carol Tavris, Pam Mendels.

For beginning to enlighten me five years ago as a result of rare and extensive research and personal study on her part as to the situation of the only child, I am very grateful to Marguerite Krebs of Ann Arbor, Michigan.

For a tireless effort to let us all know that "onlies are OK," I am grateful to Judith Kunofsky, an only child.

Very special thanks to Janice Palmer and Jean Lyons and Lynn Marks, to Johanna Atwood and Valerie Bottenus—it's your book too.

And thanks for much help and patience to Betty Kelly, Pam Auerbach, and Carole Stoddard.

As usual, without Nancy Cox, who is willing to listen to questions and problems or even recitations of chapter drafts by phone after midnight when both our husbands are asleep, I would never have made it.

*To my father
and my husband,
and for Johanna Cox,
Johanna Atwood and Valerie Bottenus*

Contents

Introduction
"The Spirit of St. Louis"

At twenty minutes after 10 P.M. that night, suddenly and softly, out of the darkness slipped a gray-white airplane so small and so light that only hours earlier its pilot had lowered it to hover ten feet above the ocean, calling from his open cockpit to ask a fisherman on a small boat, "Which way is Ireland?" Among dozens of the brave and adventurous who had attempted to fly from New York to Paris at a time when an Atlantic air crossing symbolized the far reaches of human possibility, only this flier had attempted the crossing alone—and only he had succeeded.

The small plane landed.

In a sense, the entire world was waiting.

That day, the *New York Times* had answered ten thousand inquiries about the flight.

That afternoon, twenty-five thousand French men and women had massed expectantly at the east edge of Le Bourget airfield.

By the time the arc lights went on at twilight, an additional seventy-five thousand had joined them around the airfield's perimeters, watching the sky. From time to time, rockets rose and burst in bright colors.

As the small aircraft, which had been designed by its pilot, touched ground, those who had been keeping vigil in near silence went wild. Lines of soldiers, ranks of policemen, and stout steel fences wilted before an irrepressibly excited crowd determined, as it seemed, to keep this hero "airborne" by carrying him on shoulders around the plane, around the field.

Newsmen, unable to hear a word from the aviator in this tumult (other than, someone thought, "Well, I made it"), would describe his modest, boyish smile; would rush to their teletypes within the hour to compare him to Lafayette and Joan of Arc; draw symbolic parallels between this event and the Armistice of 1918; ask, "Has any such ambassador ever been known?"; see him as a "God-sent messenger arriving at a critical moment, smiling faith at a skeptical world"; speak of his scientific knowledge, superb courage, ideal physique, sterling character, and unparalleled valor; conclude, "A nation which breeds boys like this need never fear for its future."

And beyond this wildly cheering crowd waited others: half a million would line the streets of Paris; *four* and a half million would wait along New York's avenues to toss eighteen hundred tons of confetti from the heights of buildings on the day this hero returned to his home country in what still may remain, despite the Bicentennial, the largest celebration America has ever known.

Later, the youngster who had been called "Daredevil" and "Lucky" would be called "Ambassador" and "General," would work with Nobel laureates and heads of state, would achieve a prominence that would not fade with the next sensational headline. In these his first moments as the hero of the world, he already symbolized to all within reach of a wireless a spirit of achievement that transcended both national boundaries and natural ones. "I've never chosen the safer branches of aviation," he had said. "I've followed adventure, not safety." With that spirit, one human being, alone, had conquered air and ocean. And millions of human beings everywhere would cease to believe in the impossible.

On the shoulders of stranger-friends at Le Bourget sat a young pilot from a simple background whose life story had been—simply—the fulfillment of a dream. Who would have thought or dared to classify him and his kind as spoiled or selfish, underdeveloped or overindulged, neurotic or un-realistic or maladjusted, doomed by circumstance of birth order to vague psychological "disease"?

None but a small yet potent group of Western psy-choanalysts and sociologists.

Charles Lindbergh was an only child.

Not every only child is a Charles Lindbergh, a Hans Christian Andersen, a Leonardo da Vinci, a Baudelaire, an Antonia Brico (though all of these were only children).

But usually, only children *are* superior people.

A dozen studies in the United States show only children to be superior in intelligence—and these studies are confirmed by others in such varied cultures as Russia, England, South Africa, Ireland, India, and the Netherlands.

Only children are not only brighter but are consistently described as "most admired" and "most popular" by peers.

They tend to develop creative imagination and exceptional language skills early, and maintain these talents.

They are *more* (not less) cooperative, and *less* (not more) "spoiled"! Teachers report them to be more sharing and courteous. The fact that only children are "thought" to be spoiled or maladjusted arises less from reality than from the envy of the rest of us, according to impressive psychological opinion.

Actually, counselors and educators of long experience observe the most "spoiled" birth orders to be:

—only boys in families with two or more girls

—last-born only girls in families with two or more boys

—any long-awaited last-born in a household where the mother's role definition is exclusively maternal

Only children, who generally learn to deal with others through negotiation and reason, are *not* the most spoiled.

Though widespread disillusionment with parenthood has been given widespread expression recently, parents of just one child express disillusionment less often than other parents. And no wonder. For *parents* of an only child are special too. As Albert Ellis wryly comments, "The secret of the only child is that he has parents who are bright enough to have an only child." Besides, in infancy, only children acquire basic socialization easier and sooner. In middle childhood, they show exceptional adjustment, autonomy, and good behavior. In adolescence, they are less given to superficial conformity or disruptive rebellion. Teenage only children are more likely to retain the values of their parents than to become life-style rebels.

Only children mature into responsible individuals, high in achievement but not overly competitive. They rank themselves higher in security and self-esteem than do non-onlies.

They are not lonely.

I know eight couples who have had one child by choice in recent years. Nobody conveyed to them the good tidings about only children just mentioned. (Actually, they were told just the opposite.) They simply figured out, alone, what the advantages of just one child should be.

The one-child family is extremely contemporary in a number of ways. It is suited to our mobility, our streamlined *less-is-more* outlook, our emancipated life-styles, and the urgent need to lower birth rates. But the couples I know exemplify another aspect of what the one-child family means: It means, I think, that we are beginning to value and love children.

Previously, we have not loved children to any great extent. In fact, our breathless, head-over-heels, cheaper-by-the-dozen approach to them had about it a quality antithetical to love, that is, the fragmentation of the self.

We may have been *infatuated* with children or the idea of them. As several writers have impressively argued, we may have been *dominated* by them. ("Kids' Country," as Shana Alexander has termed America.) Let's put it this way: Probably because of our *infatuation* with children we had more than we could manage and we were therefore *dominated* by them. But generally we did not love them.

We have almost always had too many of them to love. The very numbers of children in a household divided adult attention and involvement, the demands of the many preventing the intimacy among the few—*just* as it would among adults, for children are human beings too, if less developed. (I am willing to believe a woman with twenty cats loves cats. I am willing to believe a scholar with fifty first editions loves first editions. But I believe a man surrounded by a dozen women loves no one. And a woman with a dozen children loves none of them.)

Contrary to the idea illuminating the old cliché "There's always enough love to go around," there always *isn't.* Love is no mystical force, no rare atmospheric element with unlimited powers. To be sure, it has elements of mystery and inexplicability, but it grows, like any other human activity or emotion, from consciousness and time and energy. Those who love well know this, and generally love just one. Those who love children well also know this, I think, and generally keep the love within their household undivided by having just one child.

Love, of course, does not take place in isolation. If one claims to love children, it is well to back this claim with some concern for the world they will inhabit. Interestingly, one extensive survey has found not only "love between parent and child" of greater value but "concern for the future" of greatest frequency among *women who want an only child!*[1]

The only child is ushered into a special kind of household, nurtured in an atmosphere where love and attention and stimulation will not be stintingly given. He may grow up relatively free of the insecurities which plague most human beings. Certainly there is already an indication that he will grow up to be among society's thinkers and achievers.

I frankly acknowledge the purpose of this book to be to present the case for the one-child family. *This does not mean that if you have no children now my aim is to persuade you to have one child!* Not only do our times not require your fertility, your own happiness probably doesn't either. The statistics are quite clear in indicating an *inverse* relationship between fertility and family happiness, with no-child families showing up as happiest of *all.*

But like the no-child family, the one-child family has been on the receiving end of heavy disapproval. And it is that disapproval that I want to balance with some applause.

Does this mean I am admitting to a book that is not "objective"? Yes, and no.

Once in a while you may expect me to acknowledge the existence of an only child, now grown, who insists, "I hated it." Somewhere, in some chapter, I may admit that there *are* parents who divide themselves to meet the needs of many children—or that there *may be* siblings who grew up without rivalry. I will grant that babies cry—even those destined to be only children. But it is not my intention, by way of tokenism, to put on paper such facts. We've heard them all too often, stated as confidently as though the weight of history were behind them. What I want to put down are a few things we *haven't* heard before.

So when this book addresses, say, such a topic as "Pleasures and Problems of the Only Child," you may expect the "problems" to get short shrift. Why, for the sake of some pretense at objectivity, imply that pleasures and problems, advantages and disadvantages are equal? They are not. The advantages clearly outweigh the problems. And to my mind an objective approach to the phenomenon of the single-child family is only a legitimate-sounding excuse for partial capitulation to past prejudices. And these prejudices have been not only powerful but cruel.

Did I say, "have been"? Are still.

Blanket notions like "No family is complete without two

children" or "Only children always have problems" can even today stifle the impulse (or even the thought) to have an only child. Such negative notions are in fact so powerful that research reveals that *one of the most commonly given reasons for having a second child is to avoid having an only child!*

We must recognize the ambiguous and tragic character of such a motive. To undertake creation of a life *not* out of a clear and direct *desire* to create a life—but rather to ameliorate the environment of one's first-born—tacitly denies full human value to the second-born. And this would be true *even if* we could safely assume the second-born did offer advantages to the first-born just by his very presence.

Of course, we can safely assume no such thing. Sibling rivalry shows frightening potential for personality destruction, yet it is treated fairly lightly by many professionals. However, "a boy for you, a girl for me" lingers lyrically if illogically in our collective consciousness, creating an "ideal" two-child family whose father is Madison Avenue and whose mother is myth.

The myth invokes powerful pressure to conform.

And I personally was very slow to realize this.

Going through my mail one morning almost three years ago, I came to a letter that could not be easily answered with a copy of *The Baby Trap* or anything else from a growing body of literature on voluntary childlessness.

"As an outspoken nonparent," the letter began, "you claim to experience pronatalist pressure to have a child. Nonsense. You do not even know what pressure to have a child is. *Have a child.* Then feel the pressure to have a second."

I put that letter aside, and it remained "aside" for a long time. We all cling to our working assumptions. And mine had been that pronatalist pressure ended when one "gave in" and had *a* child; ergo, it was voluntary childlessness that was singularly in need of social defense.

I did, however, begin to ask around. When any remotely appropriate chance presented itself, I asked parents of one child: Was social pressure to "complete" their family with a second child all that serious? The answers quickly built into a troubling pattern. "We are happy," one couple with a ten-year-old daughter told me, "but we are not at peace. We are accused of selfishness; and because of the material advantages we can offer Sheri, she is often envied. Though we thought for a period of time our own parents had begun to understand, they have never really 'forgiven' us."

"Nobody criticizes me for having an only dog or an only husband," another woman told me, "but I have been warned that Jim is sure to face adjustment problems without siblings. I think he would face such problems *with* siblings, given what I see in other families. But there seems no way to explain."

"One couple stopped seeing us when Georgia was two," Karen and Bob Deerfield explained. "They said, 'We'll see you after you have your second.'" "You call yourselves *parents?*" another couple was derisively asked by neighbors, in the presence of their only child. Extreme or rare examples? Alas, no.

Any thinking person should be shocked. And any unthinking person who has ever asked parents of an only child "When are you planning your second?" should feel *guilty*.

The one-child family not only is easily seen to be a happier unit than larger ones, given its emotional and economic security, but is also a low-fertility life-style desperately needed now, when the warnings of the sixties' prophets are becoming the headlines of the seventies' newspapers.

If prejudice such as is found against the one-child family were political rather than social in nature, it would fill many of the prerequisites for revolutionary action. And it may even be that a "revolution" of a sort is indeed beginning.

Not all revolutions involve barricades and broadswords, manifestoes and military campaigns. Not always is there a clearly recognizable Danton or Robespierre. Though we are used to thinking of a revolutionary action as being measured by a change in government, a change of group behavior can be just as revolutionary. Sometimes, in fact, may not the most profound acts of rebellion be the least visible, at least initially?

Thousands of couples—now, this year—are quietly refraining from completing their private reproduction of the way "the American family" is commonly pictured.

This year, over 1.5 million couples will have a first child. Ten, even five, years ago, virtually all such couples would have begun thinking about a second. But something is happening. Many of these new parents will do no such thing. They will look at their newborn child and know their family to be complete.

And this fact is potentially revolutionary.

In a nation that has always been aggressively expansionist, low fertility is revolutionary. In a nation that always pursued growth, the idea that *one* is somehow *not a small number* is clearly innovative. For a nation too concerned with technological development and territorial expansion to question easy folkloric generalizations about family life, the transition from "the lonely only" to "the outstanding only" represents not a small step but a quantum leap in outlook—in short, a revolutionary change.

It's not the only revolution going on, of course. In fact, the near ubiquity of phrases like "The story behind . . ." "The truth about . . ." point to a general skepticism, a re-examination process, tacitly suggesting that we have intimately cohabited with illusions of many kinds.

Even in the sphere of family planning, the emergence of the one-child family is only part of a wide-ranging trend that may gradually overthrow pronatalist systems of thought ("Anatomy is destiny") and their institutional supports.

Heretofore we have always believed that large families were happy, were patriotic, were necessary, were loving, were *normal*. We are beginning to believe it no longer.

Many young couples so little trust the folk wisdom that has tied family to fertility that they are removing themselves from the reproductive pool completely—planning to have no children at all.

The nonparent couple is often regarded as the most radical challenge to pronatalist traditions, yet the changes that could result from a one-child family norm could be even more profound demographically, and less predictable socially. Given the high cultural value attached to parenthood, far more individuals may be expected to "stop at one" than to forgo the experience completely, thus contributing to much-needed population stabilization.

Throughout Europe during the Middle Ages, when status was attached to those who joined monastic orders and thus remained childless, voluntary childlessness might almost be said to have been popular. Just as the priests and nuns of these centuries took responsibility for the betterment of society as it was then defined (whether fervently or idly), "childfree" husbands and wives often do the same thing today and even speak of "the larger 'family' of community and society" as their family.

Other historical precedents for voluntary childlessness could be viewed, but never in the enormous experience of humankind has the one-child family been considered anything but an oddity. There are *no* historical precedents for "one child by choice."

From earliest times, the phenomenon of the only child resulted from some life plan that went awry. The reproductive machinery stalled, one parent died, the child was physically defective—and the intended *first* in a line of others that never came remained instead an *only*.

Even after the welcome advent of relatively good contraception in the nineteenth century, desired family size yo-yo'd between very rigid limits: between *two* children and *four*. There began to be those who wanted none, of course. And the only child who occurred as an accident to a deliberately childless couple began to be seen. But a couple never had just one on purpose. The only child was still due to *some* failed plan: Either the ovaries didn't work—or the diaphragm didn't.

Today, for the first time, things are changing.

Only children are becoming wanted.

In 1975, census researchers realized that the number of young married women who plan an only child had reached an impressive 11 percent—more than a 100 percent increase over the past eight years alone. Preliminary 1976 figures predict a healthy expansion over even this number. The one-child family *could become* a new family norm in the near future!

Paralleling the increasing popularity of one-child families, though not totally related to it, has been a virtual explosion of studies on "birth order." Perhaps because family scientists are just human beings like the rest of us— and like the rest of us culturally trained to value what is new —it shouldn't be too surprising to find that sociology and psychology, just like the rest of the professions, follow fads. And right now birth order is "in"—as "in" as open marriage, organic cooking, modular furniture, Cancun, or ballet.

It would be hard not to note a few excesses.

Psychologists at a recent conference were heard seriously discussing the differences between being third-born in a family of four and third-born in a family of *five*. Phrases like "That's typical second-born behavior" greeted such small acts as a request for a program change. The game even continued playfully after conference sessions ended. At one cocktail gathering it was determined that all the first-borns and only children present were drinking white wine, and all the later-borns were drinking red wine.

A study exists showing first-born women to represent the majority of a sample of striptease dancers[2]—and a study exists showing third-born women to be overrepresented in a population of Carmelite nuns.[3]

Philip S. Very and Joseph Zannini of Rhode Island College have demonstrated a statistically significant number of beauticians to be second-born.[4]

There is even a study entitled "The Birth Order of Birth-Order Researchers," suggesting that first-borns are more sensitized than later-borns to birth-order issues!

While it is tempting to smile at all this, let's not be too quick to do so. Excesses are easy to find in most fields (indeed they may predominate in many!), but that doesn't require us to write off entire occupational areas as worthless. Excellence may be rare in birth-order research (or medicine or dry cleaning or appliance repair) but it is worth seeking out, for two reasons.

First: the birth-order field has definitely turned up a good deal of solid information based on carefully conducted interviews and statistical studies of large sample populations. And research that seems solid should call for conclusions —at least tentative ones—or else its purpose is merely to gather dust, not to teach us something useful about life. I have tried of course to refer only to studies that I trust. Earlier, I did not make the generalization that "Only children have superior intelligence" lightly. Such a finding occurs consistently. And when sample sizes here are as large as 69,000 (or, in one case, consist of a survey of the entire nineteen-year-old population of the Netherlands) the conclusions they point to seem to justify faith. Anecdotal research and case histories are also valid, in my opinion, though they may await statistical confirmation. If, for example, virtually all the high school drug counselors and parents of only teens interviewed for purposes of this book believe it rare for an only child to be a problem drug user, it seems to me this should be said *now,* not five years hence when more definitive research may be available.[5]

A second reason for paying attention to birth-order research is even more basic. The entire field has as its premise something almost impossible to dispute, i.e., *our development is importantly and inevitably affected by the number of people we lived with during the time when we learned who we were.* Thus the possibility certainly exists that some personality traits and achievement potentials may be due to whether we were first-born, second-born, later-born—or only.

And in a society where choice and consumer preference

are held to be important, prospective parents talk increasingly often not only about *whether* they want children but about *what kind* of children they want!

The science of genetics, burdened as it is with ethical debates, legal problems, memories of World War II, and fears of 1984, may still someday allow prospective parents to choose whether their offspring will have olive skin, black, or fair; blue eyes or brown; be male or female. That is not the point here.

Nor is talk that "first-borns excel in sciences" the point of birth-order research.

When young people today consider having children and speak of the kind of child (or children) they hope to have, they have in mind certain general traits of character and personality.

Not long ago, one always seemed to hear women say, "I just hope the baby is healthy," but that expressed hope was inherited from a time when not many babies *were,* or could be counted on to be. Today, increasingly, young people express hope that any child they have will be not only healthy but intelligent, independent, and a valuable member of society. Possessiveness and the "old-age insurance" motive are heard of less. Gibran's "Your children are not your children" is frequently quoted by college students in discussions of future family possibilities. And often today's young couples say, "If we have a child, we hope he or she will make some unique contribution, large or small—perhaps to make the world a better place." Idealistic? Certainly. But no more idealistic and perhaps a little more admirable than the "my son will be a doctor and support me well" school of thought.

If today's couples do begin to pay close attention to the

growing evidence that indicates only children often possess desirable and socially valued traits, will the maligned one-child family of the past become the preferred family style of the future?

Current evidence suggests it.

We would do well to pay attention.

Chapter 1

The Success
of the Only Child

On a recent Saturday at Princeton, Bill Muse, the university's twenty-nine-year-old head soccer coach, directed the Princeton Tigers to an impressive victory over Yale.

In the stands was his father, who had driven in from Bloomfield to see the game. Actually, Bill's dad has been watching Bill's games since the 1955 Little League season, on through various levels of star performances in basketball (team captain), soccer (team captain), lacrosse (team captain the first and only year he played), and track.

Bill is the youngest coach ever to be awarded a Class A coaching license* by the U.S. Soccer Federation. But in college he majored in education as well as in sports, holds a master's degree, and is near a Ph.D. degree in the most difficult teaching field extant, the education of exceptional children.

*The Class A licensing program consists of twenty hours of written and field exams, and sixty hours of lectures and field demonstrations which are given over the course of seven days. The training is conducted by a designated leader of an international sports federation—in Muse's case Dittmar Cramer of Germany.

An innovator who in his first year as head coach at Princeton guided the Tigers to their best record in over a decade, he has also co-authored a book on the history, techniques, and psychology of soccer.

Bill Muse is an only child.

However, he isn't the *only* only child important to Princeton's athletic department.

Samuel Howell, director of athletics at Princeton, is an only child.

So is Jo Ann Navickas, manager of Princeton's varsity football team.

And John Johnson, the head wrestling coach.

Also Ed Ianni of the lightweight crew.

George Ligeti, who holds sweeper position on first string soccer team.

Heidi Nolte, women's basketball.

Also Glenn Christy, baseball; Lee Shelley, fencing; Pat Moynihan, track and field; Kirk Dabney, wrestling; Charlie Marshall, lacrosse; Caron Cadle, women's crew and women's crew coach; football players Bob Ehrlich and Mike Jackson and football coach Artie Williams; and Phil Langan, sports information officer, and Bill Stryker, director of athletic relations.

But the most notable only child to have put in his time at Princeton is probably recent graduate Bill Bradley, who has been in the starting line-up of the New York Knicks since January 1968.

Bradley was the best basketball player in Missouri high school history, and among the highest-scoring players in the entire history of secondary school basketball (with a total of 3,066 career points in four years). More than seventy colleges tried to recruit him, but he chose Princeton, a school that offered him no money at all. Scholarships at

Princeton are given only when there is financial need. Bill's father is a bank president.

"The best player ever to be seen in the Ivy League," according to a score of sportswriters, he won a gold medal for the U.S. team in the Tokyo Olympics (even though he was the youngest and least experienced member of the team—in fact, the only undergraduate), and that was almost matched by another highlight: after scoring 41 points at the end of a much-publicized Princeton-Michigan game at Madison Square Garden in late 1964 he was given "the most clamorous ovation ever given any basketball player, amateur or professional, in Madison Square Garden."

While still in high school, though, realizing that basketball was a winter sport and that left three other seasons, he filled his time by becoming a straight-A student, member of National Honor Society, student council president, and president of the Missouri Association of Student Councils. "Everyone looked up to him," a classmate recalls. "He was sort of inspirational. Basketball was one-millionth of what he could do."

A history student interested in politics, he has worked for Governor Scranton, spent time investigating Washington realities. And the same year he won the Olympic gold medal he was elected a Rhodes scholar and has completed several years of postgraduate study at Oxford.

He's gotten to know athletes of other nationalities over the years, and to know them well. Once, his compassion for the rigidly policed training and life-style of Russian basketball players he'd been talking to almost made him feel noncompetitive toward them. (The solution? "I had to pretend they were Yale.") Like Muse, he has written a well-received and well-reviewed sports book.

The *New Yorker* called him a "polite, diffident, hopeful, well-brought-up, extremely amiable young man who at twenty-one seems neither older nor younger than his age."

He teaches a Sunday school class every week at the First Presbyterian Church and belongs to the Fellowship of Christian Athletes.

"Easily the most widely admired and best liked student on campus," mentioned the *New Yorker*.

He has broken dozens of sports records, won many academic honors.

He may study law.

Some might immediately suspect the existence of this "cluster" of only children in the Princeton sports department to be born of two well-known and obviously wedded circumstances: Princeton is an Ivy League school; and only children supposedly come from privileged backgrounds. Therefore, is any high achievement among this cluster due to birth and background—not onliness?

But more than half of Princeton's undergraduates receive financial aid through scholarships, and the athletes mentioned represent a very wide range of backgrounds. Bill Bradley's father is a bank president, yes; but neither of Bill Muse's parents graduated from high school. Glenn Christy's father is a New York City transit policeman. And George Ligeti, whose father brought his family from Hungary to Calgary, Alberta, when George was fifteen, worked as a general laborer (his mother was a seamstress), recalled such lack of luxury as "a total absence of 'real' sports equipment . . . times were very tough. Sometimes we would make a 'ball' out of an old sock stuffed with paper." Artie Williams, the head football coach, recalls from his childhood "the struggle for survival of the black middle-class family."

In fact, the *majority* of the athletes mentioned came from nonaffluent backgrounds. Having grown up in the generally economically difficult postwar years, many of those interviewed say they *now* recognize their childhood situation to have been somewhat disadvantaged. What is interesting is that at the time they were growing up they did not feel any sense of deprivation—none.

What is also interesting about all these athletes is that they are not athletes *exclusively*. They are also serious students, and often serious organizers and leaders too. They are exceptionally well adjusted, as well as exceptional. They are simply more successful than most others in the field they have chosen to emphasize—and as only children they seem distinctly overrepresented in that field.

This may not seem too surprising to anyone who remembers the discovery on the part of *Time* and *Newsweek* in 1969 that a disproportionate number of America's astronauts were only children. That fact caught someone's attention when it turned out that the three members of the first Apollo crew to reach the moon (on Christmas Eve, 1968) —Frank Borman, James Lovell, and Bill Anders—were only children.

Further investigation then disclosed that no fewer than *twenty-one* of the first twenty-three astronauts in space were either first-born or only children.[1] (Even the exceptions, *Newsweek* noted, were not truly different: Donn Eisele's older brother died in infancy, and Michael Collins was thirteen years younger than his older brother. Both, for all practical purposes, spent their childhoods as only children.)[2]

It seems that one can look at any field, almost at random, and find that:

1. If the group surveyed is a group of select or distinguished individuals, there will be an overrepresentation of only children, or
2. If the group is not entirely composed of distinguished individuals, the most outstanding members of that group will still be only children

One study of teachers, for example, indicated that family size had no apparent relationship to being a *good* teacher, but only children predominated among those with the *best* teaching records.[3]

A study surveying cover personalities of *Time* magazine during the years 1957–1968 found 58 only children among the 215 men, and 7 only children among the 36 women. (Since in the general population only 5 in 100 adults are only children, those figures represent, respectively, overrepresentations of 22 percent and 15 percent.)[4]

The contemporary arts critic most often noted for literary excellence, John Simon, is an only child: so are others in the field of criticism, including Clive Barnes, Archer Winsten, Rex Reed. And two top designers (Pierre Balmain, Rudi Gernreich) are only children—as are three of twelve award-winning space scientists as listed by the 1975 Associated Press Almanac (Kurt Debus, Frederick Ordway, and Willis Hawkins) and creators of such contrasting musical styles as Burt Bacharach and John Cage.

Among Pulitzer Prize winning reporters, one thinks immediately of James Reston, Merriman Smith, Walter Lippmann (all only children); and approaching *any Pulitzer category* within *any particular decade,* one will almost surely find two (an overrepresentation of 15 percent) and very often four (an incredible overrepresentation of 35 percent) to be only children: playwrights Edward Albee and Frank Gilroy, poets Elizabeth Bishop and Alan Dugan, general nonfiction writers Erik Erikson and Edwin Way Teale, fiction award winners John Phillips Marquand, Upton Sinclair, John Hersey, and Robert Penn Warren.

Several survey mailings were conducted recently for purposes of this book to determine the number of only children among samples of outstanding individuals in several fields. A General Achievement list of 3,000 was randomly selected from *Who's Who*. Smaller samples were taken from a Social Reform list (consisting of boards of directors of eleven social reform organizations); a Women in Business list (drawn from *Business Week*'s evaluation of outstanding women in the business world); Arts and Letters (winners of citations awarded by the National Institute of Arts and Letters/ American Academy of Arts and Letters); and Sports (summer Olympic games, 1976).

Only children were overrepresented in *all* categories, as indicated below:

Field of Achievement	Sample size (no. of respondents)	No. and percentage of only children	Percentage of overrepresentation
General Achievement	2,150	455 (21%)	16%
Social Reform	112	34 (33%)	28%
Women in Business	71	12 (17%)	12%*
Arts and Letters	59	15 (25%)	20%
Sports	50	16 (20%)	15%

*The "Women in Business" figure may be slightly lower because there are doubtless *fewer* only children who are females. If a first-born child is a female, many couples are wont to "try for a boy."

Any investigator who begins to look at the situation of the only child will be cautioned by the first few people he or she interviews that not too much weight can be given such statistics. Why? Backgrounds again. The theory goes that since it is the "best and the brightest" couples who tend to have only children, it is privileged circumstances that animate achievement, light the fires of greatness. Circumstances of wealth or birth or education may play a role in some of the categories mentioned, *but not all.* And Alice Ginott is among those who mention how often they have seen only children become extremely accomplished, even given a nonaffluent early environment and seemingly poor circumstances and minimal abilities.

Two examples of only child "clusters" from unprivileged backgrounds come to mind.

One story was told to me by a man who immigrated to America in the late 1930s with four of his cousins. Young and enthusiastic, if not outstandingly educated (only one had attended college at all, and she had not graduated), on the voyage to the United States they thoroughly discussed the advantages they planned to give their *own* families when they married. The optimum number of children to have was discussed. Eventually, a consensus was reached that *one* would be the most propitious number. Over the following eight years, each of the five cousins married. Each had one child. Where are those five only children now?

1. Female, 34. Married, no children. Columbia degree in journalism. Editor of two community newsletters, credits as researcher on two books. Tutors at several schools on volunteer basis, organizes feminist rap groups. Income from free-lance articles (on family life or medical subjects) around $12,000.

2. Male, 38. Pediatrician in large midwestern city. Married, two children. University lecturer, a fellow of three medical societies. Income last year in excess of $60,000.

3. Male, 30. Sculptor. Graduate UCLA and several design schools. Lives in California but travels regularly to Hawaii and Far East. Has several definite design "styles" for different galleries, dealers. Income varies but is large enough to support this life-style and regular political, other donations. "Almost married."

4. Female, 32. Grants officer for large foundation. Previously traveled for State Department as information officer for AID. Salary not stated but "very comfortable." Lives in East Side apartment, maintains upstate New York home for widowed mother, whom she partially supports. "Almost married."

5. Male, 34. Graduate Harvard Business School. Partner in international investment banking firm. Salary $50,000. Married, one child.

With one exception, salaries are all above $20,000. Without meaning to imply that income is the most important criterion of success, it was definitely *one* important hope and goal held in mind by the parents of these five children. This income level, plus their parents' conscious planning for educational opportunities, seems to have resulted in the kind of security the parents hoped their children would find. All also report they are "doing what they want," consider themselves happy and adjusted. They all maintain close relationships with living parents.

Another interesting "cluster" consists of twenty-eight individuals held together in a friendship network in the Southwest (mainly in southern California, around Los Angeles). Ranging in age from sixteen to almost eighty, most of these only children met at some point during their schooling, though not always in the classroom.

Most of these only children live within commuting distance of Los Angeles (although two have second homes elsewhere, one near Vail, Colorado, the other a small weekend apartment in San Francisco). All are black or Chicano. None came from wealthy or even college-educated families.

Nonetheless, *all* could be termed successful. One woman now heads a college library department at Stanford, another woman was recently appointed as assistant district attorney for a large San Francisco Bay area county. One man has built, "from the ground up," an employment agency, another owns a large machine rental business. One manages investments, another manages hotels. Several teach. One adopted girl whose natural mother was syphilitic and who was born facially deformed graduated from high school with good grades and now owns a crafts gallery that is prospering. Almost *all* of these twenty-eight individuals, as described by a correspondent who is at the "center" of this cluster, credit what they have been able to achieve to the fact that they were only children—or were raised as only children!

In an interesting article entitled "Childhood Background of Success in a Profession," Philip J. Allen chose a profession to study in which "success" would be measured by salary but not *only* by salary; he was also interested in a profession in which relationships with many people were important, and in which clearly defined values had to be upheld. The field he chose to study was the Methodist ministry. The group of ministers *most* highly rated according to all criteria contained the greatest number of only children (with only children hardly showing up at all in the group evaluated as least successful).[5]

Dr. Sylvia Wassertheil-Smoller believes that parents' expectations and encouragement play a major role in preparing only children for success. "If you have high expectations set for you, you will rise to them," she says.

And certain qualities of only children well prepare them for adult success.

Health and energy are only-child attributes. A typical father wrote of his nine-year-old only daughter, "She goes on ambitious mountain climbs without complaining of tiredness, hikes endlessly. Other kids moan, complain, then quit. She'll hang in forever."

Reinforcing such descriptions was the January–February 1974 issue of the United Nations publication "Development Forum," in which the physical superiority of only children was well documented by Dr. E. James Lieberman.

Evidence also comes from the preponderance of only children in sports and in such highly rigorous occupations as that of astronaut. Without separating first-borns from onlies, two students of pain reactivity, in a study of U.S. Army volunteers, found soldiers from small families better able to tolerate pain than soldiers from large families.[6]

A health-care investigator in 1971 found that as family size increases, the *total medical expenditures per family* decrease! It appears then that larger families may be depriving themselves of medical care in order to meet other needs. Only children are less likely to face that privation.[7]

In 1964, a study of twenty-five thousand illnesses in a group of Cleveland families, involving medical records, physical examinations, and lab tests, revealed an increased incidence of contagious disease with increased family size.[8] Adequate, good nutrition has also been widely observed to directly relate to family size in all but the top socioeconomic groups. Thus only children definitely have health advantages.

Intelligence. "My daughter spoke three hundred words at eighteen months. It was very exciting," reported one mother. Princeton coach Artie Williams recalled, "I skipped kindergarten because I was able to do everyone else's work after I finished my own. I started first grade when I was five. Later, I skipped the fourth grade. I started college when I was fifteen."

Such only children are exceptional—but not *atypical.* Only children show consistently superior scores in intelligence and reasoning, to the point where a decision to skip a grade is often made at least once during the school career of an only child.

As early as 1953, a classic study of over ten thousand children in Scotland provided the clear finding that only children scored higher on intelligence tests than did members of sibling groups. At age eleven, the average IQ score for only children was 105, and for children from larger families, 90.[9]

Other studies have shown differences of as much as 22 IQ points in some comparisons; and in 1958 the *Journal of Teachers of Education* reported, "The child without brothers or sisters has been shown to make the best academic record in high school. *All other factors were nonsignificant"* [emphasis mine].

A sample of 4,195 English and Welsh children ages seven and eight was examined. Intelligence was found to decrease with increased family size.[10] Intelligence and grades in schools were negatively related to increased family size among 1,400 Asian high school students.[11] Among British ten-year-olds a severe negative correlation between IQ and family size was found.[12] In Ireland, verbal reasoning decreased with increased family size among a large sample of Irish Catholic children.[13] In Greece, intelligence was tested within four samples of children, with consistently poorer results as family size of the children increased.[14] In a sample of Baltimore births, it was found that risk of mental deficiency increased with number of siblings.[15] In a 1965 survey of 69,000 South African students, the 4 percent who were only children rated superior in intelligence and personality; and when in 1973 the entire male population of the Netherlands was given a comprehensive battery of tests (including language, arithmetic, mechanical comprehension, perceptual speed, and nonverbal intelligence) as part of a military evaluation program, children from large families ranked at progressively lower levels as family size increased.[16] Similar tests given to all men called up for military service in Sweden during one year produced the same pattern of superior scores for those from smallest families.[17] This seems sufficient for a safe conclusion that only children generally have richer intellectual potential.

Good character traits.   In a carefully conducted study of junior high school students in 1930, six to eight teachers rated their students at three intervals over the course of one school year. The only children in the group were found superior not just in intelligence, but in

    courtesy
    truthfulness
    industry
    initiative
    self-control

cooperation
dependability
health attitudes and habits
personal orderliness
conformity to law and order
fairness

Since family backgrounds were controlled for in this study, it might be mentioned that background differences were not great. On the Barr occupational scale (ranging from 0.00 for a hobo or derelict through 20.7 for an Edison-type inventive genius) the range of occupations of the fathers of only children spanned 6.42 to 17.81, the range for fathers of siblings 3.62 to 17.81.

The authors of the study were quite certain of the validity of these ratings, concluding at the end of their paper that "The only child is *definitely superior* in marks received in school, health attitudes and habits. . . . The only child is *quite certain to be superior* in personal orderliness and cleanliness, initiative, self-control, industry, truthfulness, dependability and courtesy, the odds being 19 to 1 in his favor. . . . The only child is *also higher* in IQ, cooperation, and conformity to law and order, the chances being 9 to 1 that he is superior. . . ."[18]

Leadership. Social psychologist Toni Falbo, after concluding comparative research on only children and non-only children, noted that only children belonged to fewer clubs and organizations than first- or last-borns, but they were every bit as likely to be officers: "They tend not to be joiners, but leaders," she commented.

Further, she wrote, "When I looked at the extent to which these students were willing to diverge from the group's decisions, I found that only children differed far more often than the others. I had the chance to pursue the leadership question at the Center for Creative Leadership in Greensboro, North Carolina. A cross-section of teachers there filled out extensive test batteries in the course of their training. As the teachers tried to reach a group decision, observers rated them on several elements of good leadership:

> whether they were articulate,
> offered good solutions,
> showed initiative,
> defined the problem clearly,
> motivated and influenced others,
> and led the discussion.

We found that only children and first-borns scored higher than middle- and last-borns in leadership."

Two European studies described by Walter Toman in *Family Constellation* confirm leadership results: In one, only children were found most frequently elected spokespersons of their high school classes; in the second, they predominated among the leaders in youth organizations. Toman devotes a little time speculating as to why: Though the high frequency of only children might at first be surprising, he explains, "single children may be recognized among their classmates as less involved in, and less threatened by, the sundry rivalries that prevail in their classes," and children with siblings less able to deal with such rivalries.[19]

Sharing, cooperativeness. "Her lack of possessiveness continues to amaze and delight," wrote a French adoptive mother of an Oriental only child. "She never seems to regret having given away her toys to other children. If, cradled in my arms, she says, 'Je t'aime, Maman,' she always quickly adds, 'Et toi aussi, Papa.' Nowadays, if faced by one of those asinine questions posed by adults, such as who-is-your-special-friend, she answers, 'Tout le monde,' and if pressed for specifics she says, 'I have twenty friends.' There are twenty-one children in her class."

Dr. Falbo's studies also found only children to behave in more cooperative ways than first- or last-borns.

Parents of only children responding to questionnaires wrote frequently:

"shares"

"less spoiled than others"

"gives nicest toys away or loans special toys"

"teaches younger children"

"voted most unselfish in eighth-grade class"

In fact, compared to a control group of parents with two or three children asked to respond to this questionnaire item, parents of only children were more than three times as likely to consider their child unselfish, sharing. Typically, one mother wrote, "When my son was four he stayed with my sister. A little boy from across the hall visited her apartment and played with my son, seeming to particularly enjoy a fire truck my son had taken with him. The next day the same playmate returned, and my boy immediately went over to the fire truck. (My sister thought it was to take possession before the other child could.) He removed some smaller toys from the top of the truck and wheeled it over to the visitor. Though this was some years ago, the same unselfishness and consideration for others persists."

Dr. Falbo wonders if this behavior is often seen "because only children, who grow up without constant competition from other children in the family, learn to trust the motives of other people." Dr. E. James Lieberman offers an even simpler explanation: "You can give more freely when you have enough. You can be charitable if you have always felt well treated, not deprived."

Adjustment. Bruno Bettelheim wrote, in *Truants from Life*, "It is often thought that the only child is more likely to suffer from emotional disturbance than the child with siblings, either because of his parents' concentrated attention upon him or because of his lack of play companions. This theory does not hold true for children who are so severely disturbed that they must be placed in the School" [for emotionally disturbed children].[20]

This was consistent with the findings of a study conducted six years earlier by Dorothy Dyer, who found only children of college age to have better emotional adjustment than sibling groups.

More than three-fourths of sixty-two psychologists surveyed at the 1976 annual meeting of the American Psychological Association considered only children "as well as or better adjusted" than others, as did Grace Langdon and Irving W. Stout in their 1951 book *These Well-adjusted Children.* Dr. Alice Loomer concluded for *Parents* magazine in March 1967 that the only child "is a happy, well-rounded child," and Dr. Falbo, after her research, offered further confirmation of the normal adjustment patterns of only children: "Students without siblings scored well within the normal range of American college students on two scales of personality adjustment. . . . Another study of 217 older adults produced the same results. People who had been only children, regardless of their current age, were no less well adjusted than anyone else, as measured either by the kinds of jobs they chose or by a second extraversion/introversion scale."

Marguerite Krebs has observed that only children are less likely than children from larger families to exhibit the most common adjustment problems that cause classroom disruption and trouble for teachers at the elementary level. They (the only children) are less likely to be bullies; they seem less likely to be hyperactive.

As a sidelight of research done for another purpose, the Institute of Social Research at the University of Michigan compared only children to those with siblings in terms of *efficacy:* "Efficacy" might be loosely defined as a sense of self-confidence, or control over one's own life. As measured directly by such questions as "Have you usually felt pretty sure your life would work out the way you want it to? Or have there been more times when you haven't been very sure about this?" only children scored *higher* on a scale of 15 by almost a full point than non-only children.

"Efficacy" seems close to what C.E. Osgood and others undertook to measure earlier, in 1957, by the similar name of "perceived potency." In the Osgood study, too, only children scored consistently higher than the norm.

At Princeton in 1965, Morris Rosenberg supervised a large survey to measure the "self-esteem" of 5,024 junior and senior high school students by means of teacher-administered questionnaires. Only children were found to have the highest self-esteem, especially among boys. (Male Jewish only children scored conspicuously high.)[21]

In income and educational attainment as measured by the Institute for Social Research, only children again rated at the top. Only children completed an average of 13.7 years of education (compared to 12.4 years for non-only children) and earned in 1975 an average hourly rate of $7.02 (compared to a $5.85 per hour average for non-onlies).

But the most meaningful mark of the "success" of the only child is no one simple criterion: not dollars earned, years of school completed; not "efficacy" or orderliness or even popularity. "Success" might rather be considered the sum total of all these things, plus a characteristic pattern of wide-ranging interests. There is a certain *multidimensionality* usually seen in personality that makes it inadequate to view only children just in terms of high accomplishment—as Nobel Prize winners, honor students, or star athletes.

When Ed Ianni came to Princeton and filled out the requisite freshman forms, it took him awhile to complete the job. In addition to an impressive athletic history of high school awards and honors, he listed the following:

Straight A's for all four years of high school
Class valedictorian
Scholastics award
Forensics award
Mathematics award
French award
President of French Club
President of Speech and Debate Society
First in state finals in speech and debate
National Honor Society
Student council
Who's Who Among High School Students
Society of Outstanding American High School Students

Society of Distinguished American High School Students

Echols scholar

Angier Biddle Duke scholar (including scholarship to Oxford)

First place Alliance Française State Contest

Third place Philadelphia Historical Society Annual American History Youth Award

and recreational activities—"writing, philosophizing, rock concerts, dances, hiking, weight lifting, charity drives, golf, swimming, going often to the beach, listening to music."

Ianni's record is not that exceptional when compared to biographies of others among this group of Princeton only-child athletes. In fact, it is *typical.*

Everyone in the group listed academic honors: dean's list, honor roll, "straight A's," National Honor Society, National Merit Scholarship finalist, Connecticut scholar, valedictorian, salutatorian. *Everyone* in the group held leadership or service positions: class committees, class or student council officerships. *All* listed extracurricular activities and recreational activities other than sports: music, drama, technical production, newspaper, yearbook, photography, science club, Future Teachers of America, glee club, debate. (There were a few unexpected touches: Though Bill Muse jokingly refers to himself as a "soccer chauvinist," his interest in sports includes the psychology of sports, with its interweaving elements of discipline, leadership, cooperation, competition, and his interests extend as far as poetry and mystical philosophy. Mike Jackson is an avid collector of science fiction. Bob Ehrlich is an excellent musician.) Several among the group are student activities coordinators or resident dorm advisors. Several are students in the Woodrow Wilson School of Public and International Affairs and look forward to careers in government service, or social reform in the private sector—and their potential looks outstanding. (Leonard Shecter of the *New York Post* began a column by saying, "In twenty-five years or so our presidents are going to have to be better than ever. It's nice to know that Bill Bradley will be available.")

All are greatly admired.

A sportswriter who visited Princeton's athletic department and met this group, knowing they were only children, described them with the following words: "I've never seen a group so cooperative, articulate, warm and friendly, enthusiastic, happy, sociable, relaxed," adding as an afterthought, "and in such excellent physical shape." There was also, she noted, "a sense of optimism that was almost tangible. You could see why these people were popular. Somehow being around them makes *you* feel better." Caron Cadle may have put it best. "People say I'm a Pollyanna type. I take things easy. I know I'm a success. And I'm thankful."

Parents of only children often used the word "balance" in responding to questionnaire requests for descriptions of their child. "My husband and I have one child by choice," wrote an upstate New York woman. "She is the most perfectly well-balanced child one could imagine. An IQ of 160, a student at the School of American Ballet, she loves animals and books and travel and clothes and classical music and has many, many friends. She is very loving and considerate and does not have a 'spoiled' bone in her body."

A father from North Texas wrote, "It's not *just* that our boy out-performs any other ten-year-old in the classroom

. . . it's not *just* that he's always chosen for spelling teams . . . it's not *just* that he's built up the biggest subscriber list of any paper boy in our town . . . it's not *just* that he finds time to 'help' the fire squad with incoming calls one afternoon a week and still finds time to play baseball . . . it's the way he manages to balance all these things and more into one small life that shows no end of interest in everything."

The correspondent who wrote at length about, and distributed questionnaires among, the twenty-eight only children in the southern California "cluster" described a similar well-roundedness, aliveness. Exerpts from lengthy sketches include:

LOUIS: Ambitious, hardworking (works for the telephone company), belongs to Kiwanis, likes sports, motorcycle riding, politics, reading, traveling. His mother lives close by but is most independent. Many friends on and off the job. Very popular in community.

PAUL: In administration, married to Francie (also an only child). Four cousins, only one of whom he sees often. Friends are "family." Has received awards for his job, also for summer teaching, swimming, silver making. Also travels, gardens. Quiet, universally liked.

SUSAN: Excels in grad school. Many interests include baseball, art, electronics, cats, poetry, swimming.

LYDIA: In her mid-70s. A very warm person, excellent sense of humor, very creative artistically, enjoys swimming, music, reading, travel, and keeping up with the talk shows. Though she is surrounded by ultraconservative friends, she just keeps getting more liberal. Just recently registered Democrat for first time in her life. "Adopts" friends of all ages, her house is always full.

My correspondent added, "What I love about all of these people is their interests. I could go on and on about Lydia, how politically akin I feel to her, how in spite of age differences I enjoy hiking with her, visiting, talking, listening to classical music . . . but that is the way I feel about *all* these twenty-eight people."

One could claim that my correspondent might not be an accurate observer, not clinically trained to make psychological assessments. But I am inclined to trust her ability to count (numbers and variety of activities, accepted by those who *are* professionals as one evidentiary factor in a balanced personality), and trust as well her judgment as to the likeability of these people, since in all cases *she* likes them, and that seems a very personal and reliable test.

Even were that not so, her observations only reinforce many, many other interviews, observations, and self-reports.

My own questionnaire respondents were not only "successful" in a business-professional sense (one was Teacher of the Year for five successive years; another, a career navy officer, listed "a bushelbasketful of medals." There were White House Fellows; actresses and councilwomen; recipients of Presidential Citations for Public Service, Nature Conservancy awards, community awards, honorary degrees, and the like to the extent that many respondents had to attach extra sheets to their questionnaires) but in the creative and varied use of their leisure time ("Weekends, my wife and daughter and I hike, mountain climb, and ski. We also take in a Sunday jazz concert, art show . . .").

Success often was consonant with lots of formal education—just as often, it *wasn't.* One exporter and writer said, "I had no college but have done satisfactorily. In the army I won a silver star, two bronze stars, commendation medal,

Purple Heart, and four battlefield promotions. I have since been Junior Ad Man of the Year, Ad Man of the Year, with a special award given for television commercials I produced on location in Europe. I am a founder of SoCal Export Managers' Association, have received about a dozen Sierra Club and Alpine Club awards."

One young woman artist whose art education was limited to night school received the Governor's Conspicuous Service medal in 1970 and has begun to combine her own work with "finding talent in others, helping others get started, representing not only the graduates of art curricula but craftspeople, young and old, in institutions. Their work is often begun as therapy and handicapped by limited materials, but they often have something to say."

Somewhere there may be only children who live in ivory towers or dark garrets, who shun neighbors, have no telephone, never entertain, and have food sent in twice weekly. Somewhere there may be only children marked by monomania, not multidimensionality, whose only hobby may be, say, an isolated game like chess and whose only social interaction arrogant outbursts at chess tournaments. Somewhere there may be only children who simply do not get along with people, and (fair enough) are not liked by people in return.

But, going to great lengths to locate or hear about such individuals, I found a very, very few. Importantly, I think, they were older, and the reason *why* they were only children may well have been unintentional or unfortunate and thus their upbringing unusual enough to produce a love of isolation. And *even* then, their relative solitude still went hand in hand with enviable achievement of some sort. They exemplify (but are not sufficiently numerous to justify) one half of a dichotomy popular until recently among psychologists who studied the only child—the "shy genius" whose counterpart was thought to be the "show-off."

Along with "old maid," "fussy bachelor," "slow Southerner," and a host of regional, ethnic, and life-style personality stereotypes, the only-child stereotypes are now facing severe re-evaluation as psychologists now not only *acknowledge* the general life success of the only child but rush to produce theories to explain it.

Such theories of course center on the emotional security and relative economic security that "come with the territory" for an only child. One intriguing additional element proposed by several psychologists is that the only child can easily develop an almost unerring *view of what is real* that is the basis of all mental health. This develops from a continuing need to differentiate between what a child *experiences to be real* and what he or she is *told should be real,* in a process that might be accurately described as flowing from "an internal negotiation between what seems . . . intuitively correct and what the constraining forces of tradition . . . require."[22] Why might the process occur more easily for the only child than for the child with siblings? Perhaps because such reality distinctions are presented more often to the only child: The only child may simply experience *more* contrasts between his life as it is—and as popular legends tell him it is.

At least a few of these contrasts are predictable.

As one example, football coach Artie Williams has been *told* something throughout his life (from classmates at all-black Dudley elementary school in North Carolina to present-day Princeton) that he does not *perceive* to be true. "Even today when people suddenly find out that I don't have brothers and sisters, they change. Even when they have known me and talked to me for months beforehand . . . now, all of a sudden, they say, 'Oh, you must be spoiled.' They seem to think this is the response you should have to an only child." It contrasts with his own *experience,* however, since, "It's just not true that I was spoiled. My parents couldn't afford to spoil me. Once when I was in college I was going on a football trip. And I didn't have any money. I called home to ask if they could send me $10.00. What I got was a check for *$8.42.* They had deducted the price of the phone call."

The small but often-repeated clashes between what only children *are* and what others *assume* them to be may provide an unparalleled education in the nature of reality.

But without waiting for any formal presentation of such theories, an entire generation of young Americans is reaching its own conclusions. More and more young couples who decide on parenthood are having one child only. They have looked around at only children they have known, thought of those they may have envied, evaluated the quality of "brotherly love" between siblings and decided, along with Marianne and Jack Langham, a newly married couple in Detroit who wrote to me, "If we want to have a super child, we'll have an only child."

Chapter 2

The Joy of
Being an Only Child

"I don't want to fight with you," she said.

"Hah."

"No, really. It's just that you're still my little sister and I really think you've gotten off on the wrong track! I mean you really ought to stop writing and have a baby. You'll find it so much more fulfilling. . . ."

"Maybe that's what I'm afraid of."

"What do you mean?"

"Look, Randy, it may seem absurd to someone with nine children, but I really don't *miss* having children. I mean I *love* your kids and Chloe's and Lalah's, but I'm really happy with my work for the moment and I don't *want* any more fulfillment just now. It took me *years* to learn to sit at my desk for more than two minutes at a time, to put up with the solitude and the terror of failure, and the godawful silence and the white paper. And now that I can take it . . . now that I can finally do it . . . I'm really raring to go. I don't *want* anything to interfere right now. Jesus Christ! It took me so long to get to this point. . . ."

"Is that really how you expect to spend the rest of your life? Sitting in a room and writing poetry?"

"Well why not? What makes it any worse than having nine kids?"

She looked at me with contempt. "You don't know a thing about having kids."

"And you don't know a thing about writing." I was really disgusted with myself for sounding so infantile. Randy always made me feel like five again.

"But you'd love having kids," she persisted, "you really would."

"For God's sake, you're probably right! But you're enough of an Ethel Kennedy for one family—why the hell do we need any *more?* And why should I do it if I have so many doubts about it? Why should I *force* myself? For whose good? Yours? Mine? The nonexistent kid's? It's not as though the human race is about to die out if I don't have kids!"

"But aren't you even curious to have the experience?"

"I guess . . . but the curiosity isn't exactly killing me. Besides, I have time. . . ."

"You're almost thirty. You don't really have as much time as you think."

"Oh, God," I said, "you really can't *stand* anyone to do anything but what you've done. Why do I have to copy your life and your mistakes? Can't I even make my *own* damned mistakes?"

"What mistakes?"

"Like bringing up your children to think they're Catholics, like lying about your religion, like denying who you are . . ."

"I'll kill you!" Randy shrieked, coming at me with her arms raised. I ducked into the hall closet as I had so many times in childhood. There were days when Randy used to beat me up regularly. *(At least if I have kids I'll never make the mistake of having more than one. Being an only child is supposed to be such a psychological hardship, but it was all I ever wished for as a child!)*[1] [Emphasis supplied.]

Dr. Teresa Marciano of Fairleigh Dickinson University has often used a dramatization of the above passage from Erica Jong's *Fear of Flying* to demonstrate to feminist consciousness-raising groups how threatened the domestic, maternal woman feels by her professionally oriented younger "sisters."

Recently, she has used it to illustrate an important way in which the sibling conflicts we experience as children can linger in our adult memories—and erupt into our adult lives. "We may think we have forgotten about the rage felt against brothers or sisters when some 'minor' injustice occurred ('He was bigger and could beat me up' . . . 'I was older but I couldn't stay up later')," she explains, "but either the rage was not so minor after all or it was, after all, not resolved. It not infrequently surfaces, triggered by someone who is again trying to 'beat us up,' or deny us something we feel rightly ours. The fact that therapists see such incidents so frequently ought to tell us that sibling rivalry doesn't teach brothers and sisters how to *deal* with rivalry at all. It just gives them practice in getting angry at each other."

Dr. Marciano is one of a number of authorities interviewed who feel that sibling rivalry is highly overrated as a civilizing device—and much underrated as a problem. Though she herself was the last-born in a family of three children who always played and worked lovingly, she considers her situation atypical, and states flatly that "The idea that brothers and sisters get along is one of the great myths of all time."

Her viewpoint is a new, but not isolated, one. Dr. Charles Arnold of the American Health Foundation also calls the phenomenon of fraternal friendship "largely myth," and most of the psychologists surveyed at the 1976 fall meeting of the American Psychological Association termed sibling rivalry "nearly universal," and serious or destructive sibling rivalry a more common situation than sibling harmony.

Further, more than half those surveyed felt that childhood conflicts were not smoothed over or forgotten in adulthood; that adult relations between siblings are often surface, minimal, or "obligatory" in nature and can quickly turn to strife when responsibility for caring for older parents must be allocated, or inherited property shared. "I believe I've almost always seen rivalry, jealousy, greed, and pain when there are two or more," said one psychologist who was herself an only child.

Dr. James Lieberman, former chief of Child and Family Studies for the National Institute of Mental Health (NIMH), questioned the pronatalist values that have biased professionals in the past. "We've regarded the problems of sibling rivalry casually, but jumped on the problems of the only child as unusual and even pathological. The situation may be just the reverse, if we take a fresh look at the links between family size and the total range of family *malaise.*"

Joyce Halstedt, director of women's studies at the University of Delaware, wonders whether sibling rivalry does not present one sphere, at least, where sexual equality has existed. "Sisters have always competed just as fiercely as brothers—if more covertly. It's easy to think of masculine examples in literature or in life. Look at the plays of O'Neill, or the slashing quality of the fraternal competition shown in *Fire and Ice,* the biography of Charles Revson. But the feminine examples are there too, and it would only take a few minutes longer to think of them." She mentions the "aggressive, almost cutthroat" competition between two sisters for a department chair in a university near hers, concluding, "Females may have been socialized to be gentler, less competitive, outside the home. Inside, sisters fight too."

Alfred Adler, the man who brought us the inferiority complex, usually considered part of the great trinity of psychological thought, bridging Freud and Jung, has called rivalry "the most obvious aspect of our social life," and suggested that the goal of being conquerer results from "our training in early childhood, from the rivalries and competitive striving of children who have not felt themselves an equal part of their family."[2]

And Kathleen Norris, no psychologist but a writer of introspection and sensitivity, has written in her memoir *Family Gathering,* "I want to place my own considered theory of the main causes of human behavior beside Freud's and those of Freud's whole school. The abiding genesis of the way we act is based on jealousy. Jealousy and sex frequently intermingle, but jealousy comes first, starts earlier and lasts longer. I have seen it in babies of three months and in centenarians of 101."[3]

Few babies might have anything to feel jealous of at age three months, but the arrival of a new baby brother or sister into a household inevitably prompts what the experts call "dethronement," and just as inevitably results in feelings of insecurity. Perhaps these feelings are tacitly acknowledged by the following passages from Dr. Spock's classic *Baby and Child Care* (3rd edition):

> A great majority of young children react to a baby's arrival by wanting to be babies again . . . they may even want to be fed from a bottle. . . .

> One child admired the new baby politely for a few days then said "Now take her back to the hospital. . . ."

> When she [the mother] sees him [older child] advancing on the baby with a grim look on his face and a weapon in his

hand, she must jump and grab him and tell him firmly that he mustn't hurt the baby. . . .[4]

Spock and other authorities tend to agree that "dethronement" hits an older child most severely under the age of five, that jealousy of the new baby is most disturbing to these young children who are preverbal and thus have no way of expressing their hurt, jealousy, fear, and confusion.

One woman recalled her reactions at age five when a brother was born: "I felt deserted and everything seemed to grow dark and look unpleasant. Even when we returned home [from the hospital] Mother was still busy with the baby and had little time for me. I had been a happy child but now I became quiet and reserved. . . . Before that time my parents had been delighted with my singing and general playfulness. Now I was shushed when I sang. Mother was tired and taken up with the baby, who was rather frail during his first months. Before he was born Mother and I had spent a good part of each day walking or playing together. She seemed almost like a playmate most of the time. Now she would tell me to play outdoors and be quiet."[5]

Such comments are so plentiful as to fill a book in themselves: "Until two, I was happy and outgoing," a quiet, pretty blond young woman told a discussion group in Chicago last September. "I was considered until that time a 'sunny' child. My parents tell me that from the day my sister was brought home, my personality changed. I don't remember the change. I only remember being considered 'gloomy' and difficult. My sister and I have never been close." A bewildered father of four children told the same group that none of his four children had ever "gotten along. . . . That wasn't the way we thought it would be," he said.

Even Wyatt Cooper, author of an admittedly sentimental book that rosily recalls large families at a time when "Girls learned from their mothers how to sew and boys followed their fathers into the fields," owns up to the following reaction to the birth of his own younger brother with these words:

> My brother Harry was born when I was five. Up to then I'd had no problem that couldn't be fixed, but he arrived and wouldn't go away.[6]

He documents a carefully thought-out method for dealing with the "intruder":

> So Harry moved in. My method of dealing with him was sly. My purpose was to discredit him. It was not enough that I be thought brilliant; he must be thought stupid. It was not enough that I be considered of good character; his must be shown up as disgraceful. I only needed to drop a few innocent words that he didn't understand into a sentence to make him suspect he'd been insulted. I might say lightly, "Harry, I don't guess you're doing long division yet" (which he obviously wasn't since I'd only just begun it and he was five years younger) and he would, right on cue, fly off the handle and attack me with whatever weapon was at hand . . . as soon as he attacked I would wrestle him to the ground (I was, after all, considerably bigger) and calmly sit on him as he lay sputtering and spitting, red with rage, knowing that he would lose this battle twice—once to me, once to Mama. He was the one, after all, who had hit first.[7]

Cooper's problems as the *father* of two sibling rivals seem, if anything, more serious. In spite of what seems a sensitive and well-planned effort to prepare Wyatt and Gloria Cooper's first child for the arrival of the second,

> When it [the birth] happened, the wind went right out of his sails. We have a photograph of Gloria holding the new infant while Carter stands beside her with the most awful sick grin spread painfully across his face. He was . . . subdued and shocked, and we spent all our time cheering him up, showering him with attention, trying to show that we loved him as much as ever, *but he knew that he had lost that special status as the adored only,* and nothing we promised could restore that.[8]

Other photographs show the older child stubbornly refusing even to look at the younger, and Carter's physical assault on his younger brother while the infant slept in the nursery indicates just how deep and how painful his feelings of "dethronement" must have been.

An extreme case of sibling rivalry is documented by Peter J. Ognibene in a biography of a recent Presidential aspirant, "Scoop" Jackson, whose only surviving sibling is a brother, Arthur, ten years his senior.

> There has long been a gulf between the two surviving brothers. . . . In public and in private, the senator often mentions his parents (particularly his mother) and sisters and the strong, positive force they exerted in his life. But some friends of two or three decades did not even *know* Scoop Jackson had a brother![9]

Ognibene puts this estrangement down to "a case of jealousy," adding that Scoop has so completely put his brother out of his mind that "It is almost as if he did not exist!"

Thus Dr. Lieberman seems correct in his opinion that experts have previously taken sibling rivalry too lightly. It certainly seems so to anyone who surveys the most popular books on child care and guidance only to find such cheerful generalizations as "Turn rivalry into helpfulness," or "Exercise restraint and practice reassurance."

If there indeed *are* ways to deal effectively with fraternal rivalry, a too casual view of this phenomenon may have helped keep such methods undiscovered! It is equally possible that rivalry is inevitable.

Margaret Mead, lending her authoritative opinion on behalf of the only-child family, has written, "Actually a strong case can be made against the two-child family. Almost inevitably the two children are drawn into an extremely competitive relationship. Now one and now the other has the advantage in being taller or brighter or handsomer, a better student or a better athlete, more active or quieter, sunnier or more serious. *Simply by being older or younger, a boy or a girl, the two are expected to compete.*"[10] [Emphasis supplied.]

In the same vein, Dr. Murray Kappelman points out, "Even the innocuous remark, 'Do you remember when Johnny did that?' buries the younger child's accomplishments in crowded memories of the older child's. If, in addition, the younger child performs later than the older, the very act of attainment is diminished."[11] Such tacit or explicit comparisons easily lead to loss of self-esteem.

It is still possible to find experts of various kinds—pediatricians, family counselors, directors of child development centers—who believe there are irreplaceable benefits to the sibling relationship. But this point of view is coming more and more to represent a minority opinion.

Therapists are becoming sensitive to sibling rivalry as an underlying cause of personality disturbances in children. A "regression" that is typical—say, a five-year-old demanding a bottle when a new baby comes—is no longer regarded with a smile of amusement. Latent sibling hostilities are no longer seen as "just a normal part of growing up." One therapist reports being sensitized to the issue when "a ten-year-old patient seemed to dislike his brother so much that he referred to him not as *my brother* but as *this fellow.* 'Whenever this fellow is home, there's trouble,' he'd say. I found he was totally unwilling to call his brother by name."

Virginia Barber, author of *The Mother Person,* brings an interesting perspective to the plight of the first-born: "The first-born has every complaint his parents do about how babies disrupt their lives, without their choice in creating the situation. He has every right to take things badly."

Even a Gesell Institute counselor admitted to a St. Louis mother, "The best way we know of to keep brothers and sisters from quarreling is to keep them apart as much as necessary."

One little-mentioned cause of rivalry and resentment may be the premature thrusting of an older child into a quasi-parental role. Trying to perhaps follow the advice of the child-care books and "involve the older child in the care of the younger" may easily produce a feeling on the part of the older that he or she is now merely a servant to the new, reigning infant. And if an older child fulfills such duties responsibly (or merely uncomplainingly) the duties may increase—and so may the potential long-term buried angers. Susan Neisuler, Boston-area feminist and population activist, believes "No one has adequately dealt with the resentment of the older siblings whose childhoods are denied to them because they have to become pseudo-parents. And no one has dealt with the effect on younger children of being raised by resentful, occasionally abusive, seldom wise, older siblings."

Incredibly, people will sometimes ask, "Don't only children miss something *valuable* by not experiencing sibling rivalry? Shouldn't parents have more than one child, since sibling rivalry prepares you for life's competitions?" E. James Lieberman tends to respond irreverently to such questions on occasion: "That's like asking parents to invite a thief into their home so that their child can learn about life's trespasses."

"Sibling rivalry," he adds, "is not the only or the best way to teach sociability, not the best crucible for developing the ability to compete. Having a second child to 'teach' rivalry or competition is a poor reason for parenthood."

(An associate of Lieberman's adds one final word of advice. Any husband or wife who may be unsure as to whether the "dethronement" or "displacement" of the first-born is really that serious might ask what their feelings would be if they stopped being the "only husband" or the "only wife" in their household.)

Sibling rivalry is a *problem.*

Often it is a *serious problem* that interferes with development. In fact, sibling rivalry is so serious a problem that a *major* benefit of being an only child is clearly: *You do not have to endure sibling rivalry!*

Even if there is not intense competition within what one child psychologist calls the "sibling jungle," there can be a sense of physical or emotional deprivation.

A letter from the files of Los Angeles family counselor

Norman Fleishman makes its point about several kinds of deprivation perceived by its writer, a sixteen-year-old girl:

> I am tired of the word *share*. My sister is fourteen, and we share clothes. Mother buys us clothes that don't quite fit me, or her, but kind-of fit both of us. I am tired of spending my Saturday mornings keeping Mike and Jimmie from fighting, and helping mom with the piles of laundry before I can go out, and I would like to sleep late sometimes but there is too much noise and too much to do.
>
> I would like to know what tuna fish tastes like without the gloppy sauce but we have to "stretch" one big can to make a dinner for all of us. I like the way the boxed apricots look at the grocery store but they are almost $2 a box and we can't buy them.
>
> I would like to finish putting together my Aquarius puzzle but Gregory keeps hiding the pieces. I would like to have an allowance, and I would like to buy records instead of having to borrow them from friends. My friends don't come over too often because there is little to offer them at my house and it is too noisy. I know I should love Frannie and my little brothers and sometimes I do, but I would not miss them if they hadn't come along. *Sometimes I wish I was an only child.*

The closing words of that letter prompted Dr. Lieberman to comment, "We often are told that only children express a desire to have brothers or sisters. How often does the opposite occur—how often do siblings wish to be onlies? Furthermore, we may hear about the desire for siblings a little more often than we *should.* It's expressed because it's culturally accepted, even expected, for onlies to want siblings. They might be thought 'selfish' if they didn't and want to avoid that negative social valuation. It's certainly safer to accept at face value the feelings of children who say they want to be onlies. At least in our present state of thought we can be sure such an expression *doesn't* come from social expectation, from saying what will please people."

Wanting to be an only child is not at all rare. The phrase "unconscious desire to be an only child" crops up regularly in discussions with psychologists and psychiatrists.

Though Dr. Albert Ellis pointedly commented, "It's *not* an unconscious desire at all. It's very conscious. Everybody would rather have been king of the mountain, Queen of the May, when young. Everybody would rather have had the exclusive attention, material possessions, and fewer rules that go with being an only," a number of counselor-reported incidents can be interpreted as overt *manifestations* of a desire (whether the desire itself is conscious or unconscious) to be an only child.

Children's drawings viewed as projective techniques are a universally accepted language of inner feelings. Many times children with siblings, asked in a kindergarten or preschool class to draw a picture of their families, will draw a picture of a mother, a father, and *one child.* They will point to the child and say, "That's me." I first heard of this type of drawing from two midwestern women who worked with young children: Marguerite Krebs of Ann Arbor, and Delores Ann Hudson, then of Chicago, in 1962. But I have heard the same story many times since, and I've heard it of children of both high and low birth order, some with only one brother or sister (though more often of elder children who remember when they actually *were* "the only one in the picture" of their family).

Other manifestations of a desire for onliness include: a ten-year-old with five siblings constructing something resembling a "room" in the basement of his Fort Worth, Texas, home, and inviting *only his parents* to come to "his room"; a sophomore girl student "adopting" one male and one female teacher in the science department as her "parents" (this girl came from a family of seven children and her parents were unaware that she even had a special interest in science); a Boy Scout troop leader in many significant ways relating to adult Scout council leaders as their "only child." Details of these and other counselors' histories of boys and girls retreating from their real home, which included siblings, to a "make-believe" home and pretended parent-only child relationships would be variously interpreted by Freudian, neo-Freudian, and post-Freudian analysts to indicate many unresolved conflicts besides sibling conflicts. But the mainstream of contemporary *non-*Freudian psychological thought would be satisfied to take these incidents at face value: indicated in each case was a *rejection of siblings,* and a *replacement of parents* with parent figures who could be more trusted not to acquire other children.

Somehow, children with siblings often feel displaced enough to experience real emotional deprivation and a consequent insecurity. Such children can try to compensate by (a) pretending any brothers or sisters they have do not really exist, or by (b) supplementing the affection, attention, approval they need to maintain their self-esteem from sources outside the home.

That children with siblings feel deprived was indicated by C. Keith Connors of Harvard University, who concluded, after a comparative study of only children, first-borns, and second-borns, that the only child feels *least* deprivation in terms of affection . . . the second-born feels *most* deprivation of those three groups.[12]

And Dr. Stanley Schachter of Columbia University found, comparing only children to other first-borns among female college students, that the only children were more secure, less apprehensive, in response to the threat of severe shock.[13]

Perhaps Massachusetts child psychologist Julie A. Cleare put it most succinctly by saying, "Sibling rivalry just puts a great burden on everybody. It is, simply, *exhausting.*"

It certainly is. One can imagine the energy young Wyatt Cooper expended in trying to devise the strategies to make his brother seem unacceptable; one can without too much difficulty imagine the emotional strain involved in trying to "adopt" other parent figures.

And the way in which sibling rivalry can prove most exhausting is in its ability to stimulate a compulsive competition. Forer states in *Birth Order and Life Roles,* in comparing male only children to male first-borns:

> The male only child, like any other male first-born in a family, is likely to receive special pressure and encouragement by his parents to achieve along lines that will enhance family status. Nevertheless, *the male only child does not seem to acquire a drive for achievement that is as tense and driven as that of many older or oldest children* [emphasis mine]. The older or oldest child not only wishes to conform to his parents' requirements for him but he also desires to compete with his younger siblings. The only child relies on the advantages given him by others and *quite comfortably* in most cases moves toward achievement as the result of them. . . . Often this relatively relaxed attitude in the work situation is an advantage for him because it enables him to enjoy and be enjoyed by his colleagues.[14] [Emphasis supplied.]

In a word, the only child can enjoy a more natural adjustment.

Other sources too report the only child to be more easily and enjoyably adjusted, less intensely competitive. Dorothy Dyer, for example, concluded almost thirty years ago that "Only children at the college level seem to be as well adjusted as non-only children when the total scores of the Bell Adjustment Inventory are compared for women [college] students. In the 'Home' and 'Emotional' areas of the Bell Adjustment Inventory the only children showed a somewhat *better* adjustment."[15]

Though the older studies regarding adjustment speak somewhat cautiously, with phrases like "at least as well adjusted," "about equally well adjusted," or "slightly better than," the most recent reports are more unabashedly enthusiastic. With particular good humor, Eda LeShan writes,

> Phyllis seems shy and quiet. She draws away from the group—she doesn't seem quite ready to play with more than one child at a time. Ronnie is obviously a leader—the other boys seek him out to direct their dramatic play on the jungle gym. He's full of ideas and seems to know just how to handle the others.
>
> We decide that he probably has several brothers and sisters and that accounts for his easy sociability. We also make a quick judgment about Phyllis: she must be an only child who hasn't learned to play with other children.
>
> There is only one trouble with these observations. Phyllis has two younger sisters and Ronnie is an only child.[16]

E. James Lieberman reports that nursery school teachers find only children to be less "clinging" and dependent. Merl Bonney of North Texas State Teachers College found only children in elementary grades consistently "best adjusted," "most popular."[17] A Philadelphia eighth-grade teacher with twenty-two years' experience in three subject areas who is the parent of an only child wrote, "Though I have a certain dislike for the word 'popular' it does indicate adjustment in a superficial way. It is a word I hear others use constantly now that my own daughter has entered junior high school. She's not pursuing popularity, and she makes no compromises, but she is looked up to, copied, admired, sought after—a social leader with no effort on her part. I'd expected she might have some adjustment problems in adolescence because she was an only child: but now that my worries proved groundless I find that I'm not surprised. I tried hard to give my daughter feelings of security and self-worth and I seem to have succeeded. Further, seeing the admiration that comes her way has made me think back on how many other of the most popular girls I've seen come through my classrooms have been only children—*looking back, I find that quite a few of them were.* And, again, the more I think about it, the less surprising it becomes."

Toni Falbo, in her research comparing only children to others, found the only children more likely to show leadership in groups. Relating leadership to adjustment, an associate of Falbo's terms leadership "adjustment in excess—without time lost worrying about adequacy, popularity, status, and adjustment, there was *time* for leadership."

Only children are more likely to *feel* adjusted than individuals with at least one brother or sister. Of questionnaire responses received as part of research for this book, 83 percent of only children indicated that they felt "more satisfied with self than others I know" (only 70.5 percent of respondents who were not only children said they felt this way); and in a very similar question, only slightly rephrased and intended to check the validity of the first response, 85 percent of only children said they were "more satisfied with total adjustment" than they believed others were—and, indeed, of the "others," only 66 percent felt themselves to be "more satisfied with total adjustment than others."

Why haven't only children been popularly believed to be well adjusted? In the past, their difficulty in adjusting may have been complicated by their very rarity (supposedly, in the past, *no* one had an only child on *purpose*); it's also possible that other qualities of only children have simply overshadowed their relatively good adjustment.

For example, a quality that most are quick to attribute to only children is *intelligence.* In fact, "egghead," "bookworm," "brain," are words all too commonly associated with onliness.

While intelligence is thought to be a nice thing to have, excessive intelligence is distrusted. It's considered not only antithetical to good adjustment (according to reasoning which must go something like "Most people are normal and adjusted"; "most people are not brilliant"; "therefore brilliant people are maladjusted") but to go hand in hand with an excessively *competitive* nature.

Most studies do show the only child to be superior in intelligence (one researcher even coined the phrase "primogeniture of intellect," since later-borns score progressively lower on basic IQ measurements), and a recent series of papers from Robert Zajonc of the University of Michigan offers an interesting theory to explain why.

Children born in large families and in rapid succession are at a distinct intellectual disadvantage, according to Zajonc, which could explain why the "baby boom" of the mid to late 1940s caused the "IQ slump" to show up fifteen to twenty years later, reflected in lowered college entrance scores. (He predicts an end to the slump around 1980, when children from smaller families begin taking their SATs.)

According to Zajonc's theory an individual has an absolute mental ability that increases with age until adulthood. (It would be more accurate to think of the units in Zajonc's theory as "wisdom units" since what is meant is not strictly "IQ" but a more diffuse and encompassing measurement.) Each child is born into an intellectual environment that is the *average* of mental levels of *all family members*. For instance, if each of two parents has an intellectual level arbitrarily assigned for purposes of example at, say, 30 units; and if this couple has a baby, the baby possesses in infancy o units but "shares" a total family environment of 60 units and thus "receives" 20 $(30+30+0=60)$ $(60 \div 3=20)$.

A second child coming into this home would enter a less enriched intellectual environment. If a second child was born when the first had attained perhaps 4 units, this second child would "share" a total family environment of 64 units and "receive" 16 $(30+30+4+0=64)$ $(64 \div 4=16)$. With each additional birth, there is further dilution of the intellectual environment that nurtures the child's developing mind.

Zajonc notes that his definition of intellectual environment is "obviously a simplification of what is an enormously complex process," and certainly other factors affect intelligence. Yet the remarkable—startling—thing about the Zajonc theory is that large scales of evidence weigh in its favor. Four different studies, ranging from 100,000 to 800,000 participants, support his premise and correlate positively with family size, *even after* adjusting for differences in income![18]

The birth-order–intellectual-achievement correlation, however, is not a rigid, predictable scale of:

only children—highest measurements
first-born—second highest
second-born—third highest
third-born—fourth highest
etc.

The pattern holds up consistently,[19] except for a reversal of the two top categories: Only children generally score a little lower than other first-borns.

Why?

Zajonc's theory that the only child may have a slight disadvantage in reaching top levels because he lacks a younger sibling to interact with in a "teaching" manner seems a little feeble.

An alternate explanation was perhaps best summed up by Joyce Halstedt at an APA session where the Zajonc theory had been discussed: "The first-born isn't showing top development because he's been *teaching* his younger brother or sister but is rather concerned with *outdoing* his younger sibling. A younger sib may present the potential of a chance to teach—but in practical effect also provides an impetus to compete."

That "impetus" might have a rather compelling quality to an older child who felt the insecurity of displacement. Forer's observation that a first-born often seemed more "tense and driven" than an only child might bear repeating in this context.

Also expressing a definite lack of affection for the "no opportunity to teach" theory was Julie A. Cleare, who felt, "We are all operating under enough poor reasons for having a second child without adding this very pretty but very questionable notion that a second will provide the first with a 'teaching opportunity'! A younger child who is *not* a sibling can give an older child a better occasion to teach, communicate, share what he knows."

Teaching is ultimately sharing—the sharing of knowledge rather than the sharing of material possessions. And Dr. Cleare believes the only child can learn to share or teach more easily than the child with siblings. The non-only has an "inescapable obligation" to share or teach, which can prompt rebellion about the entire thing. Cleare believes that the situation is too complicated by emerging rivalries for much effective "teaching" to go on.

Other authorities, in fields ranging from child development to reading theory to tests and measurements, would term the "siblings teach sharing" idea questionable. Dr. Ruth Hunt in fact calls it "nonsense." Typically plainspoken, she feels "Children actually learn to hoard, not share, when they find out another little human being has been brought into their house for the seemingly express purpose of taking half their toys, half the time."

Parents of only children are prone to report greater observed generosity and sharing on the part of their only children than on the part of their children's peers who have brothers and sisters. (Their reports check out against those of parents of non-onlies, so more than just exaggerated parental pride seems to be at work. Though children under six to eight years of age are not noted *generally* for "sharing" behavior, 48 percent of parents of only children of preschool age felt their children typically shared, as opposed to 38 percent of parents of non-only preschoolers.)

Some parents of a single child in fact mention *excessive*

generosity as a bit of a problem. The father of a seven-year-old reported, "Jimmie has always had so many toys that he seems nonmaterialistic—maybe too willing to loan or even give things away." A mother whose only daughter was given several floats, including a small, brightly colored raft to take to the neighborhood swimming pool, reports the following exchange between her four-year-old daughter and another child, age five, who said, "I wish I had a raft like that." The four-year-old thought for a minute and then said, "You don't need one—this'll be *ours.*"

Heidi Toffler, who is an only child and has one child, Karen, feels that in general only children may be "freer of striving for *things,* which can be a great comfort," but is cautious about generalizations regarding sharing ("sometimes only children share, sometimes they don't. I hoarded my toys, Karen shared hers"), and strongly feels that sharing can't be taught by being *forced.*

Only children certainly seem less apt to be subject to enforced sharing.

A Miami preschool teacher believes "Kids only share if they themselves feel they have enough. Boys and girls from larger families sometimes feel they haven't had enough. You can tell this when they surreptitiously take two or three toys off into a corner by themselves. They have to come out of the corner 'by themselves,' too, once they've figured out that it can be just as much fun with somebody else. Only children don't go off into the corner. They share automatically, because they've got enough at home. It's not so hard to understand, is it? People with plenty of magazine subscriptions at home probably don't hoard all the magazines on an airplane flight, either."

If selfishness results from deprivation, not indulgence,

then only children, who generally *have* more in the way of material advantages, should be expected to be less "selfish" than children from families with two or more children. In fact, children who were older when a new brother or sister appeared can often analyze and remember a change in themselves. "I was an only child until I was nine, when my mother brought two foster children into the house. I learned within a matter of *hours* the number of hiding places *my* (now 'our') room held, because I learned that anything I didn't hide got torn or damaged. Even crayons got broken! I changed from a nine-year-old artist specializing in pictures of horses to a nine-year-old 'policeman' chasing the youngsters away from me to the point of terrorizing them, I'm afraid."

Toni Falbo found only children more apt to make "trusting" rather than "cautious" or "competitive" moves in a game situation, theorizing that "Perhaps this is because only children don't have to worry about siblings who look lovingly at them while stealing their candy."

The absence of such worries can "liberate" a child's mind in ways that prove delightful both to the parent, and the child. Without relentless *competition,* only children are freed both for more *cooperative* and more *creative* modes of behavior. The cooperative and creative areas of the personality seem not to be pulled "underground" by need to compete.

Heidi Toffler feels "This comes from the security you have as an only child. You know who you are. You don't have to constantly compete to prove who you are."

According to reports of both parents and teachers of only children, creative activities such as painting and writing are usual "only child" pursuits. And lists of leading creative individuals of a certain life-style or birth order being, typically, displayed by proponents of that life-style or birth order, it was unsurprising recently to find a published list of outstanding only children that Zero Population Growth had gathered as part of an "ONLIES ARE OK" campaign:

Hans Christian Andersen	Shirley Jones
Charles Pierre Baudelaire	Eleanor Roosevelt
Antonia Brico	Franklin D. Roosevelt
Kenneth Clark	Jean-Paul Sartre
William Randolph Hearst	Roger Staubach
Charles Evans Hughes	Robert Louis Stevenson

to which can be added:

Alvin Ailey	Dick Cavett
Edward Albee	Claude Chabrol
Hannah Arendt	Carol Channing
John Ashbery	Van Cliburn
Lauren Bacall	James Gould Cozzens
Burt Bacharach	
Pierre Balmain	Clifton Daniel
Clive Barnes	Sammy Davis, Jr.
James Beard	Robert De Niro
Charles Berlitz	Alan Dugan
Caroline Bird	Keir Dullea
Elizabeth Bishop	Loren Eiseley
Eubie Blake	Erik Erikson
Fernando Bujones	
Anthony Burgess	Arlene Francis
	Betty Furness

Clark Gable
John Kenneth Galbraith
Romain Gary
Jean Genet
Rudi Gernreich
Frank Gilroy
Lady Lucie Duff Gordon
  (translator of Hans
  Christian Andersen)
Elliott Gould
Sheila Graham
Alec Guinness

Arthur Hailey
Lillian Hellman
Mary Hemingway
Ada Louise Huxtable

Elton John

Murray Kempton
Arthur Koestler
Jerzy Kosinski

Hedy Lamarr
Robert Lowell

Don McLean
Anna Magnani
John Phillips Marquand
James Michener
Marilyn Monroe
Lewis Mumford

Anthony Newley

Flannery O'Connor
Frank O'Connor

Al Pacino
Anthony Perkins
Alexander Pope
Ezra Pound
Elvis Presley

Rex Reed
Harold Robbins
Betty Rollin
Tony Richardson
John Ruskin
Margaret Rutherford

Buffy Sainte-Marie
John Simon
Frank Sinatra
Upton Sinclair
Jacqueline Susann

Renata Tebaldi

John Updike

Sarah Vaughan

Douglas Turner Ward
Robert Penn Warren
Walter Washington
Andre Watts
Mary Wells
Oskar Werner
Oscar Wilde

Edmund Wilson   Archer Winsten
Lanford Wilson   Jonathan Winters

Such lists could be expanded endlessly, particularly if our everyday notion of "creativity" were expanded beyond art, literature, music, and theater to such areas as nuclear physics (George Gamow, others); education (Wilson Riles, others); government, demography, or general invention.

Further, it wouldn't be difficult at all to do.

But is anything conclusive really indicated by the superior creative achievement of the only children named on such lists? Very possibly not. It's not the intention of groups who prepare such catalogs to imply superiority so much as to offer reassurance. And it's as easy to attack such a list as to prepare it. One could name an equal number of only children whom no one has ever heard of; or, sufficiently motivated, a researcher could come up with an equal number of artistic second-borns, third-borns, etc.

Still it seems widely *suspected* that the only child may have an "edge" of some kind in development of creativity.

Like love, free will, or leadership—like any other rare or inspiring human quality—creativity contains its secrets. The geneticists have failed to explain it (why does a Churchill appear? where are Mozart's progeny?); so have the critics, the social historians, and the psychologists. Not only is any discussion of its development highly speculative, but even to define what creativity *is* leads easily to tracks in sand. But it is more (most agree, across the disciplines) than mere photographic or reportorial description of what exists or what has happened. Somehow, it sees the bare facts in some original way, imposes an original mode of interpretation *onto* what exists or has happened. And this is true whether the realm is geometry or sculpture, physics or poetry.

A leading theoretician of creativity, Silvano Arieti, postulated in *The Will to Be Human* (1972) that creativity *must be fostered in childhood,* even though it sometimes does not flower until adult years. He believes six factors are necessary for creativity to develop:

aloneness

inactivity

daydreaming

"gullibility"—willingness to suspend disbelief

remembrance and inner replaying of the past

By *aloneness,* Arieti has in mind freedom from constant exposure to the "conventions and clichés of life" so that an individual and unique vision may be developed and explored. Now, certainly "loneliness" is one condition of the only child against which everyone issues warnings and dire directives ("Find playgroups—Or Else!"), but Arieti and others see a positive side to it, believing that the pursuit of gregariousness and sociability may be anathema to the creative impulse. Creativity may be in essence a lonely process: Does a work of real genius often result from a committee?

Certainly a balance is needed. But though children *do* need playmates, there may be drawbacks to constant peer (or sibling) activities and a lot to be said for an hour alone in a room of one's own. And Heidi Toffler finds the simple ability to *be* alone an important consequence of *having been* alone as an only child. She also stresses a vital distinction between "loneliness" and the kind of "alone-ness" Arieti seems to mean. "Though I was alone a lot, I never *felt* alone," she says, drawing a distinction that perhaps only only children will fully comprehend. Many only children comment similarly, "We get to know ourselves. We can be our own companions." One remarked, "This is a quality many friends envy me for having."

Johanna Atwood, a thirteen-year-old only child who lives in Flint, Michigan, has cultivated this ability—and the presence of mind to defend herself when criticized for it. "People have said I like solitude too much. They seem amazed if sometimes I would rather be alone than with them. All I can say is I am *not* going to break a good habit for the sake of a dull person!"

In fact, Johanna's ability to function when she is alone sometimes stands out in contrast to that lack of ability in others her age. "If someone says to me they would be bored or lonely if they were an only child—well, that's because they *aren't!* I have noticed that one of my neighbors, who is my age, comes over to the house all the time and complains of having nothing to do. Now, Paul has three sisters so he is used to just going along with them. When he is here *I* have to think of things for him to do! He seems lost when there is no yammering going on around him.

"One day I was reading an interesting book and didn't want to stop. Paul came over, and—*watched me read!*"

Solitude is indeed a "good habit" in terms of fostering creativity, and joins easily with a second factor mentioned by Arieti: *inactivity.* Withdrawal is not meant, nor is loafing, but simply being allowed to have no required activity. Again, there is no dearth of only children who report things like, "As an only child, I did a heck of a lot more thinking, more sitting still, than most kids." Said another, "As an only child I had more money and love, of course; more attention and books; and more being alone. This developed my imagination and self-reliance extraordinarily. It is beyond me why the vast majority of children seem to need to be constantly amused and have complicated toys."

Though he was not studying just only children, an early American patent lawyer, Joseph Rossman, studied the creative thinking of hundreds of inventors and found that their creative "breakthroughs" occurred in quiet, relaxed moments, in solitude.

Daydreaming, constantly mentioned by only children, is considered important by Arieti in producing a desire to cross the chasm between the real and the ideal. In daydreaming, you live for a while in the "ideal"—the world of the imagination. Frank O'Connor has written in his autobiography, *An Only Child,* "It is only in the imagination that the great things take place, and I had only my imagination to live in." Temporary residence in the realm of the imagination easily leads to inventiveness. One only child remarked, "I made up my own games and stories of course; you can play with dolls and tinker toys just so long. Sooner or later you've got to make your own things, because you've figured out everybody else's."

Samuel Howell, now Princeton's associate director of athletics, recalls that during his only childhood he invented dozens of games, playing them out with imaginary players. For some of them, stuffed animals he made himself represented players on imaginary teams (and leagues). For others, elaborate arrangements of cards were necessary, with complicated movements representing the acting-out of game strategies Howell ascribed to the "team" they represented.

> At about age ten or eleven [Howell recalls] I began to invent games—some could be played alone, lots were for varying numbers of players for when others were around. . . .

One of the most complicated was a war game using more than 30 packs of cards. . . . Each pack of cards represented a military or social institution of some country. Five countries would typically be involved in interactions, one called Howellonia, after my name. . . . You can imagine how much space it took to lay out thirty packs of cards among "cities" made of blocks and how long it took to draw every card in the pack! Once begun, this game usually stayed assembled for ten days at a time. But my mother and father never once got impatient or demanded that I put it away. . . .

Relatively simpler was a series of sports games based on thrown dice, with the numbers that came up on the dice being "code" for certain "plays" to be made by opposing "teams." . . .

Kids used to hang around my house to see what games had been invented. I suppose in a couple of years I must have invented thirty or so different ones.

Other only children who have become outstanding in sports recall creating imaginary opponents against whom they would test physical or strategic skills.

In line with this, Arieti sees a value to the "fantasy companions" the typical only child is thought to create for himself during childhood. "When the only child invents such a companion," says Arieti, "he imagines for the companion not only physical characteristics. He ascribes to the fantasy playmate a personality, invests him with psychological attributes and patterns of reactions and belief. Beginning with himself, he then projects likenesses and differences: how is his companion like him, how different? In a sense, he is creating literature."

Only children seem to create an uncommon amount of literature—stories, plays, poems—and often what is written is impressive, in terms of character reflection or vocabulary or structure. One college freshman recalled, "In my daydreams, I created a ruler called Cavalier (also known as Cavalier of the Roses and Emperor of the Emeralds) who began a dynasty that lasted for thirty-three generations. Cavalier ruled Terra Nova, which was a city of ten islands. I filled two hundred pages with my *Terra Nova Tales* beginning when I was eight and ending at about age twelve. . . . I don't know where these ideas came from as I hadn't read epic literature yet. Just daydreams, I guess."

Perhaps closely related to daydreaming (or necessary for it) is *gullibility:* the willingness to suspend disbelief, as though for a while to believe that what is daydreamed about might be real, or might represent some more profound reality than that presented to everyday senses. (In fact, some definitions of art acknowledge this, at least the personal definitions put forth by artists themselves: Paul Klee explained that "The artist is concerned with reality rather than the merely visible"; Juan Gris similarly remarked, "The world from which I draw reality is not visual, but imaginative."

Arieti also lists *remembrance and replaying of the past,* calling to mind many artists, particularly writers, who have done so: Proust and Joyce (who were not only children); Baudelaire and Sartre (who were). Baudelaire's statement, "Le genie, c'est l'enfance retrouvée" ("Genius is childhood recaptured") could at least be contemplated in terms of what an only childhood offers. A richly imaginative childhood "recaptured" is one thing; that narrowly circumscribed by conformity something quite different. Might the unfettered receptivity to sense impressions which is thought to be the prerogative of the child be *more* the province of the only child? The possibility seems reasonable from several standpoints.

Arieti's suggestions could be placed within the framework of French psychologist Theodule Ribot's two-phase concept of the creative process (stimulation, followed by incubation) and would seem to enhance the second phase primarily.

If only children seem favored by a personal environment conducive to incubation, it's worth asking whether more stimulation comes their way as well.

"Stimulation" devolves to sense experiences, which any child quickly begins to gather: perceptions develop (the feel of a blanket is noticed), then discriminations (one blanket is rough, another soft) and associations (a blanket signals bedtime). From such rudimentary experiences the subtleties of mental and creative activity develop. It seems reasonable to imagine that children who are given a rich stock of sense perceptions and verbal labels early in life might tend to have greater creative potential.

Does an advantage in the area of stimulation "come with the territory" for an only child? The possibility shows up in at least three ways on questionnaire responses from now-grown only children: (1) A wider variety of playthings from infancy on; (2) an earlier and more deeply established habit of reading, perhaps due in part to availability of books, magazines, and other materials; (3) a more diverse personal environment in terms of recreation and travel.

Elaborating on (3), one only child wrote, "Suburbs are supposed to be intellectually arid, and cities featureless. I was raised in what must be the most featureless city the United States has to offer, but there were trips every summer and virtually every weekend."

Another factor in the nurturing of creativity is parents' conscious efforts and ability to stimulate. By themselves, toys and books do not offer as much as when they are explained, commented on, discussed. Psychologist and counselor Herbert Robbins of New York offers the firm opinion that "It's just not true that parents' abilities operate as a constant, irrespective of the number of children. It's not true that 'If a parent can stimulate one, he or she can stimulate more than one.' Most any parent is more likely to be able to stimulate one."

Agreeing, Dr. Harry Lerner of New York even offers a formula: "The more children, the less stimulation." To stimulate a child to be creative requires, both suggest, a contrast. First, rich impressions and even possible confusion over things in the outside world; then, time alone to reflect, sort out, think over. In short, offer an interesting experience, then leave the child alone.

Expectations should not be too high, of course. (One can't take a child, only or not, to a museum, then send him to his room with a paint set and expect a Titian portrait or Monet landscape.) But the basic formula is both simple and widely agreed on. *Time to reflect, after lots of input.* What kinds of input? "All kinds," says Julie Cleare. "Concerts and museums—and frogs and puzzles."

Since creativity involves originality, exposure to novel or different forms of thought and expression could well foster this quality. Tolerance of a child's first tentative, original efforts is also mentioned often. Sooner or later taste and judgment must be introduced of course (not everything original is excellent). But Arieti and others stress that it is important for parents who want to cultivate creativity in their child *not* to stress conformity of expression, *not* to criticize. Allow an original impulse to flow, unedited, for a time, for creativity needs to be undistracted by the judgment that tends toward the mean, losing in the process extremes of uniqueness.

The "unique perceptions" or "separateness of vision" of the only child *may* be allowed to wander from the norm more often than those of the non-only child, suggest counselors George Powell and Patricia Thomas, who hold that "in a large family, a creative child may easily cause chaos or competition."

To Delores Ann Hudson I owe the "square flower" example she once used to illustrate this point to me and several other Loyola students. Before describing a creative only child she taught as a speech therapist, she asked us to imagine what would happen if a preschool child with age-close siblings drew, say, a flower that was the "wrong" shape or color: square, or green. Most of the time, of course, siblings would make sure this budding artist learned that "Flowers don't look that way," or, "Flowers don't look that way, *dummy.*" Made to feel foolish, he might henceforth only draw flowers the way they "should" look. But were the child an only child, adults around him might be more apt to accept what *he* saw and represented. They might even get out an art book and show him other unusual concepts of flowers.

If there is any danger of overpraise, most feel it occurs only in extreme circumstances. When a child becomes accustomed to a parent's appreciation, he may decide to "test" it by producing something really awful. He wants to know the parent is really paying attention to what he is doing, not just giving automatic, and therefore meaningless, nods of approval or pats on the head.

A little bit of clinical evidence indicates that the creative, novel response *can* be fostered by voiced approval to unusual efforts. Psychologist Irving Maltzman has found that unusual responses increased in a word-association test when such responses were praised.

The materials of creativity also matter, but these can be simple. A twenty-color paint set as opposed to a six-color paint set is nice; but much can be achieved with just a pencil and a pad of paper. And perhaps the most important creative clay is simply the infinitely malleable gift of *language*. Here, only children unarguably have an advantage. As early as 1937 Edith David showed that among elementary school girls only children were superior in language development —and other studies have since confirmed this. The reasons are not difficult at all to figure out: *Wider reading* is virtually always reported by only children (and if an attentive parent is not nearby to explain unfamiliar words, the use of the dictionary tends to be taught early); and only children are much more apt to be surrounded by *adult vocabulary*. The young child with a sibling may be drawn into much discussion of, say, the welfare of the household finger puppets ("You took Petey Puppet"), whereas an only child of the same age might be more apt to be exposed to adult conversation about wider welfare issues involving his entire community and presented with a much more challenging vocabulary.

Patience is worth at least a passing mention. Only children often mention that their parents allowed them to develop their ideas whether this involved spending hours reading or writing, or causing minor household confusion with the materials of art or sport. (Remembering Samuel Howell's thirty-pack card game, it's tempting to wonder how it could possibly have been developed or remained assembled with younger sibs around.)

I've said that relatively greater creative talents among only children is a "suspicion" that's as easy to run into as it is difficult to solidly support. Part of that suspicion may come from reviewing Arieti's list and deducing that only children *are* alone more, *do* daydream more—or from reviewing Ribot's theory and finding it likely that only children *do* receive more stimulation and input, etc.

It probably comes down to this: *Any* child can become creative given a certain set of favorable conditions. Only children just *may* be more likely to fall into that set of favorable conditions.

A totally unexplored area of investigation might deal with how many from a random list of creative individuals were "functional" only children, regardless of their family size. True, Mozart came from a family of seven children (but all except a much younger sister died in early childhood, leaving him in an almost-only situation); true, Albert Einstein had a sister (but her education was not emphasized and offered no rivalry or pressure or competition); true, Elizabeth Browning had sisters (but she *was* educated and had for much of her childhood a *personal* governess whose exclusive attention fell her way).

And to many observers there seems *something* unique about the vision of the only child: an unusual perspective or manner of expression. This is reported often by teachers, one of whom said, "It wasn't just a totally individual way of seeing things I began to notice in only children, but often the conviction that their way of seeing things was *right*. Maybe you can get that kind of conviction only if you have once experienced being the center of the universe."

Feeling at the center of one's universe results naturally from the kind of *parental attention* only children report receiving. Over 90 percent of questionnaire respondents mentioned this as an advantage of their childhood: "more parental attention," "more loving attention," "full undivided attention of my parents," "never having to fight for attention," "feeling what I did was important, always looked at," were almost universal recollections.

"I never had to worry," wrote one young woman, "that something I did that pleased me wouldn't matter to anybody else. I knew it would."

The only kinds of advantages more frequently reported were educational (92 percent) and material (99 percent of respondents mentioned at least one example).

Children raised during Depression years remembered music lessons, summer trips, braces for their teeth. "I had things that were almost unheard of among my friends, except for one or two only children I met in later grades. My family didn't live in a castle, but somehow I always felt like a princess." Another recalled, "It was always just as inexpensive for my parents to get an extra ticket for the theater or symphony as to get a sitter for me—I learned to love such pastimes and feel a deep sense of enrichment as an adult because of things I was exposed to as a child."

Ranking very high among remembered material advantages was *my own room* (mentioned by almost 80 percent of respondents). "My room was a place where I could do what I wanted as long as I cleaned up once in a while; it was also a place where my friends and I could be rowdy and make noise." "There were rules for the living room and the dining room," said another, "but in my room I could make the rules."

"I knew my own room was precious to me," wrote a

third, "but I didn't realize just how precious until I be-friended two sisters who had to share a bedroom. They had an invisible 'border,' like two unfriendly countries. Neither could cross that line without permission—or trouble."

Thirteen-year-old Valerie Bottenus in a letter wrote, "I feel lucky because I receive many gifts, but in more than just a material sense. I consider concern for my health, my future plans, and all the opportunities I have received 'gifts' that I am very grateful for." She adds, "Within the next few years I must decide whether to go to college or put my training at the New York City Ballet School to use and try to become a professional dancer. It is nice to know that I am going to be able to make my decision free of 'what's practical' financial considerations."

Many only children realize that greater freedom to choose schools and camps (and later, colleges) has broad-ened their spectrum of career options. Many plainly state that they feel they would not have had a college education as an option *at all* if they had had brothers or sisters. ("*No* question I'd have missed out on college if I'd had siblings," wrote a Northwestern freshman. "My family doesn't have much money.") For others, it was a wider choice of type of school or type of training that was offered.

"It didn't matter how tight the money got," Princeton's Artie Williams recalled. "I knew I was going to college. I knew whatever happened that I would have every chance."

Also ranking very high among material benefits recalled were nutrition, health benefits, good medical care. "Meal-times were very dignified at our house," one woman remembered. "There was always enough to eat, and plenty of interesting, wholesome snacks. I imagined other households were the same way. Then when I was about six,

I was forced (not invited: the bus broke down and my father couldn't pick me up from a playmate's house) to spend the dinner hour with a family of five. An average-size meatloaf had been sliced with mathematical precision—but after serving, the accusations of 'You got a bigger piece' went on throughout the meal! I was so shaken that I couldn't eat a thing. I knew when I left my untouched piece of meatloaf would be solemnly divided, and then the fighting would begin again."

Erma Bombeck may joke in an age of affluence that having an only child means "Mother doesn't have to cut a maraschino cherry into four pieces," but at one time division of a family's food was no laughing matter. "You chose plentiful foods of low nutrition," recalled one Depression-era mother, "or you sliced a roast under a magnifying glass and knew that everybody would be a little hungry."

Some food fetishes or neuroticisms can be traced to childhood competition for enough to eat, according to Rebecca Liswood and other psychologists. One family counselor, going to the theater with her grown son and his date for the evening, noted that the young woman with him was nervous all through the evening because she had forgotten to put the chocolate cake she had brought "away." "Do you come from a large family?" asked the counselor. "How did you know?" the girl asked. "You don't have to worry," the counselor replied. "The cake will still be there when we get back. No one will have taken it."

Nutrition has always represented a measure of security for a child, and the more division of food necessary, the greater the insecurity (or harm) the child might experience. There is even an interesting linguistic reflection of this reported in the United Nations publication "Development

Forum" of January–February 1974: It is said that the deri-
vation of the word *Kwashiorkor,* now used to refer to a
particular kind of protein starvation common among Third
World children, comes from an earlier meaning of the
word: "displaced child," i.e., the one who had lost its only-
child status.

Other only children commonly recall preventive check-
ups, vaccines, house calls when they were ill. One young
woman remembers, "My mother and I were shopping together one spring when I was about fourteen. I was trying
on bathing suits. She squinted at me and said, 'Sue, how
long has one of your hips been higher than the other?' I
looked and couldn't see what she meant at first. She said,
'Well, it's probably nothing.' Then she said, 'No, I think
we're going to have that checked on.' It turned out I had
a rare bone problem which could have made me a lopsided
cripple within a few years if it hadn't been detected so early.
I've often thought, that, if Mom had been busy supervising
two or three of us in that fitting room, she wouldn't have
noticed that small, small change in my body."

Personal care and personal advantages of many sorts
came the way of only children even in scarce times, and
often at the child's own preference. Margery Y. of Seattle
remembers, "I think as early as second grade, I began to
be asked, 'Would you like to learn to play an instrument?
What instrument?' 'Would you like to go out to dinner?
Where?' I gained experience making choices. I don't think
I'd have been allowed totally free choice of a musical instrument if I had been one of several children. (What if we all
had picked drums?) Nor would I have had a chance to think
over different restaurants. The decision would have been
arbitrary, say, a certain coffee shop because it would have

been the only thing affordable. Of course I knew the responsibility was mine once I chose something, so I chose very carefully. But the opportunity to do so was exciting, it taught me a lot, and it's one of the things I remember gratefully."

This sense of freedom and autonomy is reflected in other responses. "I was allowed to make my own decisions with confidence. There was no brother or sister to say, 'That's stupid,' or, 'That's dumb.' My parents, being adults, were wiser and more judicious about criticizing my decisions when there sometimes *was* a need to do so or when I *did* decide something 'dumb.' As a result, I think I developed a good sense of responsibility: by being allowed to be responsible for my own courses of action."

"I never had to worry about what others thought. I didn't give a damn about groups and conformity," reported only child Hank Curtis of Washington, D.C. "If my way of looking at things differed from 'the group's,' I just kept right on believing in my way. Even as an adult I've never had to waste any time worrying about what's 'in' or 'out,' what's popular or isn't.

"I could do what I wanted pretty much," he continues, "—choose my friends and activities. If I wanted privacy, I had it. If I felt like companionship, that was up to me too. For that matter, if I needed rivalry, I found it, and I found it for just as long as I needed it, and then I got rid of it when I didn't need it any more."

"I had wider experiences than my friends with siblings, definitely," said Susan Landis of Kansas. "First of all, I could be both a daughter and a son. So I missed nothing. I went fishing *and* learned to sew, did yard work *and* cooked. And I can do just anything now. . . . Why, if I'd had a brother, he'd have done the *boy* things and I'd have done the *girl* things. We'd each have had just half a world!"

It's not just such sex-role stereotypes that only children escape, believes Ruth Hunt, but many varieties of personality stereotypes. "Only children don't get labeled, pigeon-holed, *stuck,* as 'the smart one,' 'the slow one,' 'the math whiz,' 'the beauty,' 'the dummy,' 'the clown.' It's easier to develop a well-rounded set of interests, a multidimensional personality, a more alive outlook.

"As an only child myself, I'm not the least bit shy about saying it's the best way I could have possibly been raised. I didn't have to avoid any interest areas that had already been 'occupied' by anybody older. I was free to be myself, free to become whoever I wanted to be. And I have."

Chapter 3

The Joy of
Having an Only Child

"One is fun . . . more's a chore."

Janice Hall Bottenus,
mother of thirteen-year-old Valerie

The trend began quietly at first, some years ago. A word here, a complaint there. Then the tempo picked up. Finally achieving a regularity that seemed to rival sunrise, a theme of *entrapment* made its appearance among the colorful consumer hints, new diet plans, Gothic novel excerpts, and other perennials of women's magazines.

Personal story after personal story unfolded, yielding a frightening collective image of the contemporary female psyche: Caged by circumstance, needing to find self-worth (or at least a part-time *job*), women wanted *out*.

Let's face it: The women expressing this sense of entrapment are mothers.

And let's face it: Though the notion is that "the second child is easier," aren't the women who feel so trapped almost always mothers of more than one?

Asked if it were true that mothers of two or more felt more trapped, sociologist Jessie Bernard replied unhesitatingly, *"Yes."* Why? "Because they *are* more trapped."

Interestingly, the first essay in a book-length collection of personal stories, *Redbook*'s *Why Young Mothers Feel Trapped,* is entitled "I Didn't Like My Second Child." Interestingly too, problemed parents usually refer to offspring in the plural: "The child*ren* are driving me crazy." "How can one reconcile growth and child*ren*?" "The child*ren*'s needs must always come before mine."

Comparatively speaking (compared, that is, to mothers of more than one), are women with an only child still somewhat "child-free"? Certainly, there remain some freedoms.

"We can live where we want," say those surveyed and interviewed. "I don't have to move to the suburbs in search of space," says Marjorie Robbins of New York. "With a second child, we'd have to move outside the city, because the cost of a three-bedroom apartment in Manhattan would be prohibitive."

With an almost identical phrase, yet opposite meaning, Lisl Helms of Blue Island, Illinois, says, "I don't have to commute to the city to look for work. If I had a second child, I'd have to find a really good job, because we'd need the extra income."

Lisl isn't interested in working—Marjorie is. "With just one, I can go back to my job," smiles Marjorie. "With just one, I can stay home," exults Lisl. Though their personal desires are dissimilar, both women feel that one child allows them latitude to do what they want. For that reason, both have decided not to have a second child.

A major life-style shift came attached to the second child even before the seventies. Margaret Mead's daughter, Catherine Bateson (who now has a grown only child), remembers, "Lots of people when I was first married had only children. The minute they had two or more they moved out of New York City. No sensible person stayed in New York with more than two children. You couldn't afford it. So they went off to the suburbs and you didn't know them anymore."

". . . you didn't know them anymore."

The phrase suggests an identity shift as well as a life-style shift. Does this, too, await the second child?

There seems a general feeling among parents of one child that *just* one can be "taken in stride," lets you remain yourself, does not take over your life. In fact, fear of such a takeover is often put into plain words: "With one child, you can still be a person. It's the second one that 'locks you in,' makes you a mother," believes a River Vale, New Jersey woman, adding, "In this neighborhood at least, in the case of every mother I know, we all started tranquilizers after the second one." (She calls the neighborhood Pill Hill, and she doesn't mean that doctors live there.)

Larry Bowers, a Philadelphia salesman, had pretty much the same feeling: "We—my wife and I—are just two people. We have our lives under control. Now, our lives just might get *out* of control if we let ourselves get outnumbered."

Marian Kratz of Indianapolis expressed, "I'm still called *Marian* more often than *Mom.* That matters to me. My husband and I have a combined dislike of harried housewife-mothers, Little League, Big Bird, toilet training, active listening, constant chauffering, shopping centers, pediatricians' offices, peanut butter, hot dogs. With only one child we find we fit that pattern less." She adds, "Of course anybody who tells you there is *no* life-style change after one baby is crazy—not to be trusted. But we have found one child to be manageable: I am *not* the frustrated mum of the soap operas!"

With successive children, work increases exponentially, mothers say. Mothers of one child by choice seem quite conscious of that. "I figure I'm going to be tired for the next six years," says Kay Levin, director of social work at Planned Parenthood in Chicago. "But that's better than figuring on being tired for the next ten or twelve years, which is just what I'd be asking for by having a second after a 'proper' four- to six-year interval."

Of a woman who did just that, Dr. Teresa Marciano says, "I've seen her handwriting deteriorate; her notes to me reflect only depression."

A mother of two admits, "No matter when you plan to have that second child, you seem to lose. My friends and I have tried it all kinds of ways. If they're closely spaced, the sheer work load of *two infants(!)* is overwhelming, the laundry mountainous, the worries over health greatest. And they seem to fight more. On the other hand, if you wait five or six years, then *just* as you're ready to regain your own time again, you are thrown back to the diapers. Waiting even longer, when you've emerged not only from the diaper phase but the get-sick-and-break-things stage, you are thrown back to square one of *both* those stages again. And in this last case there is just too great a span of years out of your life given to parenthood!"

Marian Kratz considers herself fortunate to limit that "span of years" given to parenthood. But the free time on a day-to-day basis that she gains by having an only child seems a closer benefit. Marian, whose daughter is four and a half, kept track for one week of the details of her day, as did a neighbor who had both a four-year-old daughter and a nine-month-old infant. A somewhat abbreviated comparison of a "typical" two to three hours for each follows. It is presented *not* as an intended comparison of *any* mother of one child *vs. any* mother of two children (for clearly any mother with an infant is going to lack free time), but as a conscious message to those women now at the very threshold of the "proper interval" between children, who may be considering having a second child very soon.

MARIAN		NEIGHBOR	
7:00	Woke, bathed, fixed hair, got semidressed (housecoat) for breakfast, woke Bob.	**6:45**	Woke. Baby fussing in next room. Turned back alarm which had been set for 7—reset it for 8. Went to change baby, Nancy came in, also awake early, wanting "help" in the bathroom, I follow her, carrying baby & extra diaper to change him there since I don't think Nancy needs any "help," she's just acting help*less* to compete with baby, a phase. She wants to fill the basin with water, not wash her hands under the tap. Baby crying now. I tell Nancy to wash her hands the usual way. She lets out a little yell of insistence. "Don't
7:15	Started coffee, breakfast while Bob walked dog. Checked *Today* schedule in *TV Guide*—nothing. Discussed the following with Bob: political editorial, local referendum articles in newspaper, also read the comics. Also discussed over breakfast: whether he'd be late or early from office tonight, what plans to make for weekend, several household matters, new pillows for living		

room vs. new plants
for garden, discussed
new sitter (I don't like,
want to find older
person—trustworthy,
and nice to give them
the employment)
talked over sitter *vs.*
parents (his or mine)
to stay with Tammy if
we go away this
weekend; if sitter, ask
her over about 6? (why
I wanted to know if
he'd be early or late
tonight). Long range:
next summer vacation.
Tammy's to go with us
so we start now to find
cottage. If we find a
cheap one, one or both
of us can take a lit or
film course. Decision:
I'll take it *if* cottage is
cheap enough, giving
him 2 nights alone with
Tammy . . . he can
come & audit we think
when films are shown
and I'm more apt to
attend all classes—he's
in Chgo once in a while
(sometime during this
time I fixed more coffee).

8:00 Time to wake Tammy.
We both start down

wake your father." I fill
the basin for her, take
diaper & baby back to
his room to change,
scoot Nan out of
bathroom to rinse
diaper, move
downstairs to get
baby's formula, give
Nancy glass of milk
while I feed baby.

7:15 Back upstairs. Baby
usually sleeps for 1 hr.
now while I organize
rest of family. Not
today. He fusses, will
wake Carl too early.
Solution: carry him on
shoulder while I get
diapers ready for
diaper service pickup
and fill a 2nd bag with
general laundry.
Downstairs.

7:25 Start 1 load laundry,
unload dishwasher
from night before, set
table for breakfast
(plates, glasses, silver)
put diaper bag by
door, put trash outside
door. Nancy has gone
back up to her room
and turned her radio
on. Carl now awake.

hall to her room but
phone rings & I go
back to kitchen to
answer it. Jean (a coop
dayschool mom) says
Susan (also coop
dayschool mom) needs
today off for emerg.
dental work & will
need next Tues off
also; she (Jean) can
switch w/Susan today
but not next Tues; can
I switch to Tues from
Wed *next* week? Yes.
While this was going
on Bob started
Tammy's bath. We
discuss that the
jumpsuit she wants to
wear today is washed
but not ironed. Hmm.
Is there any special
reason she wants to
wear it today? It's her
favorite. Fine. You can
wear it unironed or
wear it tomorrow. It's
Mommy's favorite too
and tomorrow is
Mommy's day to lead
the day school so does
she want to wait &
wear it tomorrow.
She thinks it over,
chooses something
else.

7:30 Back upstairs, try again
to get baby back to
sleep; he's still fussing
slightly but can be left.
Carl is in bathroom so
my shower will have to
wait (there's only a tub
in children's room, we
may have a shower put
in). Back downstairs.
Make batch of orange
juice, put water on for
coffee, put bread in
oven to toast slowly
(whole wheat for Carl,
Nancy only eats the
white stuff), fill juice
glasses, put butter,
peanut butter,
preserves on table,
cream, sugar. There
may not be any towels
in bathroom—are there
any clean ones in dryer
—grab a couple from
dryer to take upstairs;
2 bath towels
disappeared when
Nancy took them to a
playmate's house to
make a "sleeping
bag"—call Sheila T.
to see if towels are
there.

7:45 or so. Almost make it
to Carl with the towels

8:30 Tammy has her cereal & fruit while Bob and I have more coffee.

8:45 Helen arrives to pick up Tammy for day school—that's Bob's signal to leave for the office: everybody out the door.

8:50 Feed dog, clear breakfast dishes, clip the editorial Bob & I discussed (to send to friend in Ky.) and clip a few cents-off coupons from food pages, water indoor plants.

9 A.M. Set alarm for 9:30. Nap.

but Nancy is in with baby so I poke my head in and she says he's wet again and "something's wrong," stop to check, he *is* wet but there's nothing else wrong, he often needs a change a 2nd time in morning after feeding, Nancy insists "something's wrong." I say there isn't, she says there is, I ask what, she says "he's sloppy," I say that's the way babies are, she was that way too and will she please take these towels to Daddy while I change the baby and what did she do with the towels she took to the Thompsons? She evidently took towel to our bedroom and left it and went back to her radio, Carl calls while I'm still changing baby, I settle baby quickly, rinse this diaper in children's bathroom, leave it in tub, will take downstairs to put with other soiled ones later before service comes by, then get Carl's

towels to him finally,
Nancy downstairs now
with her radio, calls
over news-noise that
something's burning.
(toast in oven)

8 A.M. or so. Everybody has
bread and jam. Finish
making coffee quickly,
pour more milk for
Nan, make note to
GET TOASTER
FIXED!! over breakfast
we talk to Nancy about
the towels except I
break away to go get
that last soiled diaper
but by the time I get
downstairs the pickup
has been made, I toss
it into the washer for a
hot rinse cycle, moving
1st load today's
laundry to dryer, piling
things from dryer on
top of worktable in
laundry room.

8:15 or so. Carl leaves for
work I hear something
& realize the alarm
reset for 8 A.M. is
going off.

And the day is just beginning!

We might have a rather definite impression that Marian, our mother of just one child, is going to have more free time. (And a better chance to end the day without an Excedrin headache or a Life-Swap urge.) We might be right. But, not content to leave us with just an *impression* of the situation where time, at least, is concerned, measurements analyst Dr. Ruth Hunt devised a structured approach to the two women's early morning schedules, designating each quarter-hour period of time as one of the following:

—Family-time units (includes parenting, maintaining household)

—Marital-time units (interaction between spouses)

—Free units (personal units)

—Future units (planning for time more than a week removed)

—Community units (community awareness, concern, involvement)

Marian began the day simply enough with 1 Free unit for personal care. The next 7 units over breakfast count mainly as Marital units (4) since the basic interaction is between husband and wife. There are, however, 2 Future units and 1 unit of community-oriented discussion based on the morning paper.

After 3 Family units with her daughter, Marian used 2 Free units (nap). Free units (7) and Future units (3) will occupy the rest of the morning. Had we followed Marian's schedule into the afternoon, though, we would have seen Marian almost *exclusively occupied with parenting*—Family units (20)—making Marian's total day seem to us *overwhelmingly dominated by parenting:*

Marian's day until 5 P.M. *approx.*

Family units	▓▓▓▓▓▓▓▓	(23)
Marital units	▓▓	(6)
Free units	▓▓	(8)
Community units	▌	(2)
Future units	▓	(5)

At least, we might think so until we compare Marian's day to her neighbor's:

Neighbor's day until 5 P.M. *approx.*

Family units	▓▓▓▓▓▓▓▓▓▓▓▓	(38)
Marital units		(0)
Free units	▌	(2)
Community units		(0)
Future units		(0)

Warns Dr. Hunt sternly, "The neighbor's day is what a nonworking mother with a four-year-old, who is even as I speak these words being told by someone the-second-is-easier, *may well be going back to!*"

In comparing a total of twelve paired schedules (working mother of seven-year-old only, working mother of seven-year-old plus nine-year-old; nonworking mother of eight-year-old only, nonworking mother of eight-year-old plus ten-year-old; etc.), with the only significant variable being the presence of a second child for one mother, the ratio of free time did not change that much. It diminished, in most of the cases, from the 8:1 ratio shown in the Marian-Neighbor chart to something around 5:1.[1]

One simpler comparison evaluated what two working mothers were able to do between 5:30 P.M. and 6:30 P.M.

in the evening, after their return home from work. (In both of these cases, husbands arrived home at about 5:30 also.) One mother had a five-year-old only child, the other a five-year-old and a seven-year-old.

Both mothers had the following objectives:
—take a nap; bathe
—talk to child (children)
—read the paper; relax
—talk to husband
—call friends; misc. personal
—begin dinner

Conclusions after analyzing these schedules:

1. Only the mother of the only child got her nap. Though the mother of two "sometimes" does, while husband watches children, with two children she explains that there are simply "more kids coming to the door, more doors slamming, and even at that age the phone rings often." The day sampled was not a quiet day.

2. Both mothers spent time with their children (the quality of the time was not evaluated).

3. Both read the paper, the mother of one while her child played quietly in his room, the mother of two while the two children watched TV.

4. Both mothers talked to their husbands, but in the case of the mother of two the husband went upstairs twice, briefly, to settle disputes.

5. Neither called friends as they had planned.

6. Both began dinner, the mother of one with both child and husband in kitchen "helping," the mother of two while her husband supervised the children's baths.

Marian Kratz is typical of mothers of one who explain, "In the relatively quiet atmosphere of our home, with no quarreling siblings, I can count on time to read whenever I want to."

Other parents of one similarly explain, "We are lovers of peace and quiet and of personal time. Often we share time with our child; but often, frankly, we spell one another so that we can each simply do what we want to for a while."

"Free time" might seem a shallow reason not to have a second child. (Some, in fact, might call it selfish.) Marguerite Krebs, an Ann Arbor psychologist who has specialized in studying the only child and has an only son herself, doesn't consider it selfish at all—or if selfish, then not wrongly so.

"So many people in my generation had two children, or three or four, and now view their lives as having been stolen from them," one woman told Krebs. Clearly such feelings do no one any good.

Krebs feels, "It is good for the *child* as well as the parent —and therefore *un*selfish—for a parent to keep mentally alive. This happens more easily with an only child. The child gets to know parents are people because they *are* largely people." "With two-plus kids," Ruth Hunt adds, "parents get to be 90-percent-plus parents. Given an only, they're more apt to remain 50 percent autonomous, functioning adults—not just someone who answers to 'Mom' or 'Dad.' "

While they seem to be talking about identity, Krebs and Hunt are really talking about *time,* for time available to you is necessary for you to define yourself according to some professional or personal interest. It's hard to call yourself a researcher if you haven't seen a library in years, or a painter if you no longer even remember where you put your oils.

With more free time, parents of one child more easily continue personal growth or at least maintain levels previously achieved. Perhaps the most startling research suggestion to back up this view is that a large number of children may have an adverse effect on the intellectual growth of the parents. Robert Zajonc and Gregory Markus of the University of Michigan Institute for Social Research cite complaints by kindergarten teachers who say they must regress to the verbal level of their pupils. Similarly "outnumbered," the parents of large families may suffer the same fate, they say.[2]

Every mother of an infant (even an infant who will definitely be her only child) must have moments of frustration, wondering, "Will I ever have an original thought again?" After all, her child cannot communicate and interact on an adult level; and other mothers she sees during the day communicate on a *child-care* level (which in the view of some is not quite the same as *adult*). But it is the process of *extending the phase of caring for young children, with successive births,* that can habituate a mother to a nonintellectual world, with limited horizons.

Marian's neighbor, in fact, well recognizes the frantic and unfulfilling pattern of her days, doesn't like it, admits to being surprised by it.

"No, I didn't think it would be like this . . . I thought since I was staying home with Nancy anyway I might as well have another, especially since I was enjoying Nancy so much, was so glad I'd quit work to have her. Now, too often when she wants to do something or wants attention, I'm not free. The obstetrician said the delivery of the second would be easier. Nobody said a goddam thing about what would be harder—the work, the lack of free time."

It's not just the free time as measured in minutes or hours, Dr. Ruth Hunt stresses, it's also the relative lack of preoccupying tensions that allow you to sink into that time —plan it, use it, enjoy it. "A case could be made after all that this neighbor's schedule could be juggled, shifted, streamlined according to efficiency principles, to give her a few hours to herself during the day. But she might not know what to do with the time, since she is so used to domestic activities, 'maintenance thinking.' " In fact, this emerges from the two schedules the women wrote or dictated: Their ways of describing housework and meals vary —Marian's more casual, her neighbor's more involved, detailed.

Free time in the *evenings* presents a contrast too. For mothers of more than one child such time may be less productively used or serenely enjoyed. Marian volunteered that "when Tammy is invited over to a friend's house for the evening or to spend a night, we are then without responsibilities, which we wouldn't be if we had other children at home. My husband and I are not so tired from dealing with children and jobs that we can't enjoy each other." Asked about a similar situation—when *her* daughter was invited out for the evening—Marian's neighbor merely said, "I don't do anything special—I'm just glad to be able to collapse and get a few extra hours' sleep."

A few extra hours' sleep is precious to those who bought "the second is easier" idea. As Jessie Bernard points out, the joy of parenting *one* is the joy of parenting *less:* You are not exhausted from trying to be fair to each child, trying to prevent jealousy, rivalry, or conflict.

One mother reported, "With one child, I could count on his taking a nap at some time during the day. Then I could nap too or do what I wanted. With two, I am either in the autocratic, tantrum-producing role of enforcing simultaneous naps—or while one is asleep I feel compelled to spend 'personal time' with the other. The result is obvious. I haven't had a nap in months."

Another reflected, "I notice a major difference: It's difficult for my six-year-old and me to finish a conversation anymore—he will often start to show me something and never get to finish explaining it."

"*Monitoring* yourself is exhausting," said another. "With two, you have to weigh out words of praise like grams of gold. If I tell Steve his drawing is 'good,' then I have to be careful not to tell Lorraine hers is 'very good.' Steve and Lorraine even watch my expressions. For no reason that I can think of to kick myself for, one will burst into tears and sob, 'You like her (him) best.' Then I know I haven't been even-handed enough." "And how do you ration hugs?" asked another mother poignantly.

Hank Curtis also offered the following observation: "I've seen power situations develop among friends' kids very quickly. One will dodge, one will dump on—parents I know keep really busy straightening it out."

That simple lack of "being busy straightening out" sibling conflicts can add greatly to the sense of control and pleasure parents of an only child find in their role. "We have not ever experienced the feeling so common to our friends—of being 'sick of kids,'" one couple wrote.

Very frequently parents of a single child just say, "We enjoy our child," or, "We have fun together." And such statements might seem unimpressive until one considers how rare it is to hear them said sincerely. And conversely, how common it is to read the latest survey on "Parents

Who Wouldn't Do It Over!" How frequently parents say the names of their children with tight lips, rueful expressions, shaking heads—almost with an air of what one observer convincingly compares to martyrdom.

Julie A. Cleare and Heidi Toffler both use the word "intimacy" a lot when describing the one-child family. Heidi Toffler feels that "You *understand* your only child much better. Because of competition, siblings cause 'editing' of behavior, maneuvering. Parents of an only can know strengths, weaknesses, interests—the way you ought to know the qualities of someone you love."

Cleare adds, "More intimacy is possible with one child. Parents 'speak' to one child more, not just in words but in behavior. They communicate more to the child because the child is watching them, learning from them, aware of them, learning to pick up subtleties of human behavior. The child may notice something and say, 'Mommy, you're in a hurry this morning,' or, 'Daddy, why didn't you like the news tonight?' and the parents are delighted that the child noticed. The process works in reverse, too, of course. You don't as often find parents of an only child feeling alienated from that child. They've kept in touch."

One simple index of how much more in touch with their child most parents of onlies are is suggested by Marguerite Krebs: *Only children watch TV less,* she insists, challenging any doubters to conduct their own neighborhood survey. "With one, there's much less temptation to say, 'Go to your room and watch TV.' The family stays together a little longer in the evening."

"Without pretending there's been no change from our child-free days," one woman wrote, "we are able to have our child share in most aspects of our lives, to go and see and do and be—with almost as little hassle as if there were no children."

Another, expanding on this point of view, said, "We have been able to share more, much more, with him (our son) as a result of his being our only child. Both his father and I are very close to him and share lots of time and activities. Today, with so many parents wanting outside jobs, social life, community work, recreation, education, etc., it leaves very little time for children—often *too* little time. This leads to the frustration of parents' *not enjoying their children.* I don't say these parents don't love their children: I say they don't *enjoy* them as my husband and I enjoy Steve. I am very glad I chose to have just one, can devote enough time and still have my own interests, and find, after merging it all together, that I am cheating no one."

A career choice for the mother of one, similarly, offers less conflict, less worry that somehow a parental role is being neglected. For parents of an only child, the ability of both spouses to pursue careers without domestic disruption is often considered important.

Though there is some evidence to suggest that low-fertility women may have a more traditional view of the role of mother,[3] a tendency to express impatience with the career motives of other women ("Why should I need to go out and get a job when I love my child?" demands Lisl Helms. "The mothers who can't wait to get out the door and punch their time clock have had too many children and hate them"), there are at least as many voices willing to state the case for "the best of both worlds": career and home.

Certainly, there is *some* conflict.

"It *is* a compromise," admits a Washington, D.C.,

mother of a seven-year-old. "You *do* give up parts of your ambition, little bits and pieces, holding back from your career. You *don't* have the freedom of the childless woman. But professional and domestic goals can blend. It works. Just barely sometimes—but it works. With more than one child, I don't see the two spheres blending well. They collide." An office mate who also has one child agrees. "I have gotten to know my child *well* despite my working hours. With more than one? Impossible. Some women around here say they do it. Maybe."

Certainly, the inevitable conflict of roles is *minimized* with just one child. A parent with strong career commitments may find *that in itself* reason enough to have, at most, an only child. Counselors tend to agree on this ("High-ambition women are happier if they are low-fertility women," says one), and a noted columnist has explained her decision to have an only child for this reason:

> At the time that I had my daughter, I was teaching at Hunter College and Columbia University. I also had a fellowship from the American Association of University Women and was doing research on leadership at UNESCO. When Lisa was born, I stopped these activities to take care of her full time until she was five and ready to start school. . . . I decided not to have another child because I would be unable to keep up with my profession and give a new baby the same amount of time I devoted to Lisa. Above all, I didn't want to be a mother who resents her children because she feels she has given up her life for them.[4]

But it is in the area of family relationships that parents of only children may find most profound enjoyments.

Again, *choices* are involved. Even if one's life situation is potentially enjoyable, a "no options" feeling can descend like a dark cloud and create trouble where it need not have been created.

Several examples of choices available to parents of one child showed up during an hour of back-and-forth banter in Arlington, Virginia, in early 1976. Some advantages named: "It's easier to take an only child with you. You don't have to get a sitter." (On the other hand, someone called out, it's easier to *get* a sitter.)

Unequal division of labor seemed another problem area that parents of an only could frequently skip:

—"It's easier to cope if one spouse doesn't do his share."

—"You're being sexist. You mean if one spouse doesn't do *his or her* share."

—"Nope, I mean *his* share." (Laughter.)

—"At the same time, 'he's' more apt to do his share if there's only one child."

There was agreement on the last point. Yet several felt that even "shared" child-care responsibilities could lead to a "split spouses" syndrome after a second child. "We constantly see our neighbors, each with a child, on the way to a separate car, and hear, 'I'll take Sally to her lesson while you take Bobby to do the shopping,'" observed one woman.

And while there are some errands where husband and wife wouldn't join each other even if they had an only (would they *both* have taken Sally to her lesson if they had had just Sally?), there is a wide range of activities that parents of an only child *are* likely to share (might they both have taken Bobby to do shopping if Bobby were their only?). In the latter category are many recreational activities, performances by a child that need not be missed because of schedule conflicts.

Somewhere, it should be admitted that *even one child* interferes with marital intimacy. Studies documented in three major books on voluntary childlessness make the point (as would a minimal application of common sense). Still, common sense would tell us equally well that while one child creates a strain, one creates less of a strain than two!

Of two marital "systems" (Figs. A and B, see p. 106) drawn from *The Mirages of Marriage,* [5] the all-encompassing child system is the less desirable of the two. This (Fig. B) presents an extreme situation in which the child system engulfs both marital interaction and each individual parent's autonomy. "And the more children you have, the more likely your system is to become that way," says one of the authors of *Mirages,* William J. Lederer. "Leaving aside the question of the success or problems of the only child, the *parents* of an only child have it easier. I know some great marriages with just one child."

The change from one to more-than-one child might be diagrammed another way. When *one child* is added to a relationship, *three relationships* have really been added to the basic male-female bond. (See p. 107.)

A second child would add *nine* relationships to be kept going. Obviously, the fewer children, the stronger can be the basic man-woman bond. The most ideal situation in these terms is the childless one; but the one-child family is certainly the second best.

A similar principle can here translate itself from the language of emotion to that of economics. With one child, money, like intimacy, need not be split so many ways. Fewer expenses and female career patterns are factors in

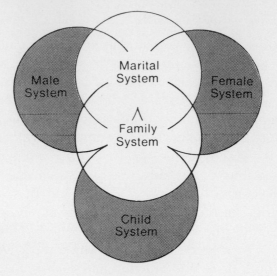

Fig. A

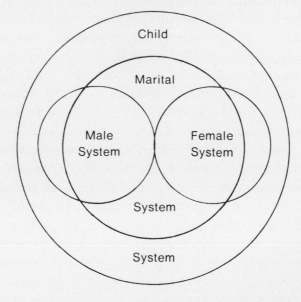

Fig. B

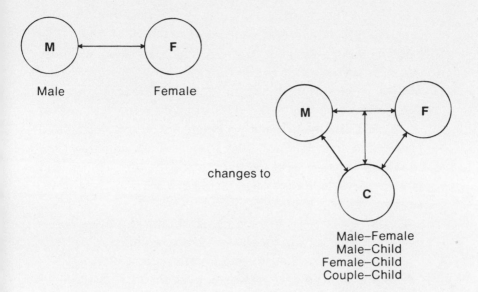

Male   Female

changes to

Male–Female
Male–Child
Female–Child
Couple–Child

the relative economic freedom a two-person employment pattern can give a three-person household.

Even one child is costly. The cost of raising even one child, excluding a college education, easily exceeds $90,000 and has been estimated at $150,000. Major sources (U.S. Commission on Population Growth, Institute of Life Insurance) imply that on the *average,* though not all years of childhood are equally expensive, out-of-pocket costs will be about $2,000 *per year* to age seventeen. Lost-income opportunity costs for one spouse then propel the grand total toward its awesome six figures. (Then, once college age is attained, annual cost of even one child can easily jump to $7,000.)

To repeat, *even one child* is not easily affordable by most Americans. But if both parents work, and only one child must be supported, lost-income opportunities can be held to a minimum, and bills paid more easily.

As an example of how this can work to the advantage of very young parents of only children, Bill and Denise reported, "Bill's salary just supported us before the baby was born. (I wasn't working, but did five years of community work for no pay.) But by the time the baby was three years old, we were several thousand dollars in debt. I got a job then, which not only covered the cost of a sitter and helped with the bills but gradually helped pay our accumulated past-due notices. We will start to get a little ahead in time to take a vacation next summer; and we'll get farther and farther ahead as long as we don't have any more children. And we do *not* intend to."

Parents of one list the following among the most *important* economic advantages to having one child:

—Being able to insure against emergencies

—Being able to save against emergencies ("If either of our cars needs new tires, we don't have to snap at each other or go into a state of gloominess," said one mother)

—Ability to avoid extended credit

—Ability to have recreational, educational opportunities for self and child

—Feeling secure about ability to finance child's education

Money is also relatively available—not just for basic needs or hedges against the unexpected emergency but for enrichment activities: plays, concerts, vacations. "It's really a little exciting," said one counselor, "to watch a couple who had intended a second child suddenly realize that *if* they stopped *now* they could live very well. The possibilities start to dawn on them. They get very happy, and I get happy for them."

It shouldn't be forgotten for a moment that financial security means more than the ability to make house and car payments. There are more subtle kinds of "purchasing power." Just as income tensions lead to budget fights and other marital tensions, the *lack* of money problems can in a sense "buy" good personal and marital balance. Money can directly affect the amount of time both partners have available. Working parents of one child are not so apt to need to court overtime; even if only one partner works, the at-home partner can often afford household help and as a result enjoy leisure time.

Without at all meaning to imply that every couple with an only child can afford to buy all they've ever dreamed of, it *is* safe to say that they will have more economic freedom than they would with a larger family. Their spectrum of possibilities is wider. They can live relatively lavishly if they wish (because they can *afford* a large house) or they can live very simply (because they don't *need* a big house). More money simply means more choices, more control over one's life, more security for one's child.

Not only is marital harmony greater during the child-bearing years for parents of only children, but their adjustment to the post-parental years is easier.

Counselors agree that an only-child marriage can minimize the often traumatic transition to the so-called empty nest. Those surveyed among the members of the American Academy of Marriage and Family Counselors agreed that though there is unquestionably a peak period of marital breakup when children leave home ("That's the morning husband and wife face each other over the breakfast table and realize they've talked about *only the children* for twenty years"), the *fewer* the children, the *less* risk there has been for such a quiet estrangement to gather underground strength. (For a couple without children, this particular transition problem does not exist at all.)

If the empty-nest problem hits hardest those parents who have had the most children, at least the closeness that comes from facing a common problem might draw husband and wife together *if* they were equally affected by the sudden absence of children. But since child-rearing in America has been the female's province, the empty-nest trauma has been primarily a *female* problem. C. Ray Fowler, executive director of AAMFC, states that the successful adjustment to the empty nest "depends primarily if not exclusively on the emotional health and stability of the *mother*" (emphasis mine). (The comparable problem for the father is less empty nest than empty career.)

The mother's problem seems to come about because gradually, without realizing it, she invests too much of her identity in the role of mother. Thus even as she says, through the years, "When the children leave home, that's when I'll begin to live for *me,*" she is concurrently forgetting how to do just that. After many years of putting the children first, her own identity becomes so deprived that it is as *unable* to absorb sudden psychological plenitude as a starved body is to absorb an eight-course meal.

Women with one child have two built-in chances of escaping such transitional difficulties. First, they have spent somewhat fewer years being mothers. Second, mothers of one child are more likely to nurture other roles during the time when they are raising their children. Their relationships to their husbands, having been less disrupted, are likely to be in better repair; their jobs or professions (if any) more established; their range of interests wider; their goals better developed.

There seems a *continuity* to the marriages of parents of an only child that is well illustrated by the following statement from a retired father of one: "By having only one child, my wife and I kept in touch with each other. Now that Nan is grown, we spend nearly all our time together. My wife gave

me a motorcycle for Father's Day and we ride in the country
to gather berries for homemade jellies and wine. But that
is only one example. We are happy. It's not that we don't
miss having Nan around. But on the other hand we were
ready to see her go.

"We'd almost been looking forward to the empty nest.
We wanted to do a little flying ourselves."

Aiding the parents-of-one in retaining a good relationship is this: *They are very often pleased with, and proud of, their
child.* Not only does this mean a lack of such no-win, extra-
innings games as blaming each other for a child who did
not "turn out" as hoped, but there is rather a shared, positive pride that a joint life "investment" has reached maturity. The odds seeming to be what they are these days
against the fruitful maturation of the parental investment,
against a child's growing up safely and creditably, one
mother remarked, "I will feel so relieved and thankful—
lucky—if ten years from now Rob is educated, established,
and doing something productive that interests him."

"Luck" will probably have little to do with it.

The process of successfully raising an only child begins
with the kind of planning that creates its own luck. One
characteristic of parents of a single child that is consistently
noted by researchers is *planning.* Parents of an only child
tend not to be "rushers into things." ("I get very annoyed,"
one confided, "with people who don't plan their lives, and
then resent us because we did.")

In particular, they plan their parenthood.

A *New York Times* story in January of 1975 reported that
of a large number of couples interviewed who had an only
child by choice, "All had planned that child."[6] And because
parents tend to plan carefully for their first child the event
seems to be happier than the arrival of any later children.

In one study, 84 percent of women during a first pregnancy described themselves as happy, while only 36 percent of mothers in second, third, or fourth pregnancies so described themselves.[7]

Thus from the very beginning the groundwork is laid for a sound family structure. One mother wrote, "Our child was welcomed with open arms by both of us. We knew he would not be a great financial strain, and both of us were prepared to give 100 percent as parents because we were to have only one chance at parenthood. He will lack nothing, including love, discipline, patience, attention."

Explaining his typical keen attention, another parent said, "With an only child you get *all the experiences* that parenthood has to offer—the first word, the first step, the first school day—but you get them *once.* So you pay a little more attention. A little thing that might be ignored in a large family is special to us because we haven't seen it before and we know we won't see it again. We don't get jaded or bored."

Reporting on recent studies, Judith Weinraub concluded, "The child who can expect the most attention from his father is the only child. Similarly, the father's interest in his children dwindled as family size increased."[8] Several other studies also underline the point that closeness, pride, and caring are characteristic between the generations of a one-child family.

"It's this way," explained a father asked to name the most important advantage he saw to having one child. "With an only child, *you tend to get the child you want.*"

That may well be. Parents want a child who is healthy (only children tend to be), bright (every environmental advantage maximizes development), and well-behaved (only children are more apt to conform to adult standards of behavior they see around them).

As adolescents and as adults, there is some indication that only children assume roles pleasing to their parents. The goal held by the five European cousins who immigrated to America in the late 1930s was primarily a financial one: They wanted their children to achieve economic security—all five of their only children did.

Other examples come easily to mind. Mary Astor's father and Romain Gary's mother may have gone too far in actually selecting specific fields of achievement for their only children—but their children achieved in those fields.

Bill Bradley's parents seem not to have pushed a particular choice of profession, but hoped he would come to possess certain hallmarks of character (A close friend of the family has said, "Susie knew what kind of a son she wanted, and she has him"), and there is certainly no disappointment there.

Firsthand and secondhand, from interviews and questionnaires, parents of an only child expressed *satisfaction,* said such things as: "There is something very special about our child." That's not so astonishing, perhaps. We all know parents blinded with pride who think that their quite rebellious or ordinary children are "special." A little more of an eye-opener is the fact that, in the case of the only child, the feeling seems reciprocal. Only children, as adolescents and as adults, *seem to like their parents.*

Evidence of this comes from several quarters.

At Wake Forest University, a hypothesis of a wide-ranging study comparing only children to others was "That parents of only children are more influential models for their children's development than the parents of non-only children."

This hypothesis was tested directly by the question, "In terms of making you the person you are today, who was the most influential person in your life?" Optional answers to the question on the printed response sheet were: close friend; teacher or authority figure; parents; well-known person, such as a celebrity.

The comparison revealed that a startlingly higher percentage of only children (40 percent) chose parents than did first-borns (3 percent), middle-borns (2 percent) or last-borns (7 percent). [9]

Though Toffler and others have spoken of the family's loss of power to transmit values to the next generation as one factor in the "fractured-family" syndrome, the only-child family seems minimally fractured.

A Department of Health, Education, and Welfare publication summarizes research based on studying almost two thousand parents of high school children simply: (1) As family size increased, adolescents perceived their parents as having a less positive effect on them. (2) Adolescents' positive feelings toward their parents declined with increasing family size. [10] Counselors Patricia Thomas and George Powell believe "The only child tends to pick up many of the characteristics of the parent to a greater extent than other children." And I have often heard that even in the critical, rebellion-prone teen years only children tend to remain fairly close to the basic values of their parents. "The best example I can give you is drugs," the mother of fifteen-year-old Jan told a lower Manhattan rap group. "She listens to her peers' ideas. Then ends up accepting mine."

Elsewhere it has been said that the joy of parenting *one* can be viewed as the joy of parenting *less*. It might be equally true that the joy of parenting one child is the joy of parenting *well*. And to many people the measure of good parenting is raising a child who accepts you, identifies with your values. This may be the greatest reward parenthood has to offer; conversely, the total rejection of their values by their young is to some parents the greatest tragedy.

"Value identification cannot exist without respect. And respect and admiration from their children is what all parents hope for. I'd even go so far as to say that the reason some parents have many children is that they hope their odds here will improve—that *one* of the bunch will grow up to admire them and grow into someone they can view as a friend," says Dr. Herbert Robbins. "But it again gets back to how parents plan to communicate their values. It *very* quickly gets back to planning. Successfully transmitting values isn't accidental."

Consistency and respect for the child are important too, along with planning, he adds. One can see how that would work. In fact, one questionnaire respondent explained it very well by saying, "We never wanted a child of ours to call us hypocritical. Since we can communicate more fully with one, there's less chance of that. If we *say* we value democracy, we want to have a fairly democratic household. The authoritarian approach large families require would then conflict with what we believe." Though the writer went on to give other examples, perhaps that one will do. And, again, the letter is typical of the parent of an only child in reflecting planning, careful thought, looking ahead. And since such tendencies pay off in many areas of life, perhaps Albert Ellis is right when he suggests that the success and special nature of the only child result from the *kind* of people who have only children: people who value children enough not to have them casually, but instead with thought and foresight.

Chapter 4

Echoes from a Past of Myth and Prejudice

The question was always asked of me, "Do you have any brothers and sisters?" When I said *no,* the answer to that was "Oh, too bad." But the questioner never explained why it was "too bad."

As a young child, I remember being at a party playing a guessing game. Someone said I was the only one in the room she was not jealous of. The others had to guess why—and the reason was that I was the only one, who, like she, had no brothers or sisters.

I remember having a book of paper dolls to cut out, and I took the book to my friend's house next door to see if she would like to cut them out with me. My friend's mother said, "You mean you brought your book to *share* with Julie? My, how unusual for an only child to share anything." It was the first time I heard the words, and I heard them in the same breath with an uncomplimentary assumption. I went home and asked my mother what an *only child* was. I was five years old.

Most only children report being made aware of their status by the time they are six years old—and usually by a source outside their own home. The adults who made the comments above say that no matter how much they came to *appreciate* their only-child status in later years, the memories of such early responses to their "onliness" remain strong.

Of two-hundred adult only children responding to a questionnaire, only nine felt they had never experienced negative feelings of others toward them. Two of these nine added marginal comments that they felt this due to deliberate efforts of their parents to spare them such attitudes through specific attempts to "consciousness-raise" neighbors and even teachers with whom they as children came into contact.

Ninety percent of those reporting negative comments and attitudes recalled the word "spoiled," often coupled with "spoiled brat."

"Selfish" ran a close second.

> "You're so spoiled," I heard constantly from classmates in first grade. What was *spoiled?* I wondered. Looking back on this constant experience the only thing I can imagine is that the way I dressed was presumed to make me *spoiled.* Now, I also wonder if my little friends were reflecting what their parents had told them MUST be true about me—i.e., "Margie is an only child so she's bound to be spoiled."

> When I was just learning to play baseball, a lot of the boys a year older than I was used to cuss when they struck a foul or were called out on a base run. Once when I missed the ball I said, "Oh, damn," like I'd heard the older boys say. And the catcher said, "What's the matter? Do you always act like a spoiled brat if things don't go your way?"

Similar remembered situations often involved an elementary school classmate's response to an only child's receiving a good grade, wearing a new item of clothing, winning an honor: "Oh, he [she's] just spoiled." "The tendency was," explained one college student, "to call all of us who were only children spoiled brats, whether we were or not."

Women who were only children seem to find the problem persisting into adulthood more than men. One young woman reported, for instance, "A man I was beginning to date, on finding out I was an only child, said, 'That probably means you're spoiled and will expect a lot of presents.' He didn't say it as if he were joking."

Such only children are not just being mildly paranoid. A wide variety of studies over a long period of time almost tells us there is a *reflexive* association between being "only" and being "spoiled" in the general way of thinking. Norman Fenton in 1928 found that the trait most frequently attributed to only children was "spoiled";[1] the Department of Health, Education, and Welfare in 1974 found the most common reason women gave for not having an only child was "Child will be spoiled."[2]

Since the accusation of being "spoiled" seems nearly universally remembered by only children during their childhood (almost a "red flag" response), one might well ask just what it means, and why it is made.

Elementary and secondary school teachers who were asked indicated clearly that "spoiled" and "selfish" were accusations directed most commonly to only children (rarely to children with siblings) *if* it was generally known that the child was an only, and seemed to diminish after early elementary grades.

As to the underlying meaning of this personality attribution, opinions varied, but no teacher queried believed the opinion of other children to be unerringly correct.

One said, "It's often a simple case of jealousy finding an

ego-saving device"; another, "When the accusation is spurred by a material benefit the child—usually an only child—has received, the underlying assumption seems to be that since this [only] child has such nice things he must *demand* such nice things. Ergo, he is 'spoiled.' "

Often, of course, the only child has quite innocently received something nice and has not "demanded" it at all. In fact, a number of parents who nonchalantly gave their children such things as new sweaters, sneakers, notebooks, and matched pencil sets noticed their children consciously "dressing down" after the first few days at school. "Like Jo in *Little Women,* when she went away to school," said one mother, "my Frances had new clothes of many colors, but after the first week of school preferred to wear the same denim jumper day after day." Frances may sensibly have been responding to an unwritten dress code. Or maybe somebody had called her "spoiled."

In their research on only children, Sharryl Hawke and David Knox asked scores of non-onlies if they thought being an only child was an advantage or a disadvantage. Those who considered it a disadvantage (a majority), when asked to explain, most commonly gave a reply involving the term "spoiled brat." Onlies were characterized as demanding and selfish.

"Only children never have to give and take; they just take, take, take," complained one of Hawke's interviewees, in a remark that had a familiar ring to all twelve elementary school teachers this author interviewed.

Remembering an almost identical comment he had heard from a fourth grader, one teacher said he had explained, "I don't know if only children just take, take, take . . . maybe instead they just *have, have, have.*"

This particular teacher, with many years' experience,

continued, "I really feel that, if anything, only children I've taught have been less grasping, less selfish, less spoiled, than other children. Either they're making a conscious effort *not* to seem so or they are open and sharing as a result of feeling secure in their possessions. I wonder if the thing that makes children open and sharing is feeling sure they won't be left with nothing."

I think it worth mentioning that the entire concept of "spoiled" disturbed several counselors and family health professionals with whom I spoke. In the opinion of Dr. Charles Arnold of the American Health Foundation, "*Spoiled* when applied to a child is often an anti-child word. Used by an adult, it can easily reflect the thinking of someone who inwardly doesn't like children and therefore vaguely feels that deprivation and sacrifice are 'in order' for them or needed to prepare them for a hard world. When another child casts that term about, the child may feel inside, 'Nobody is giving *me* that much.' "

Suzanne Gronke, a psychological counselor in private practice in Plantation, Florida, agrees. An only child herself, she recalls, "All my life I've heard that I'm spoiled, that I've always gotten what I wanted. It used to make me very defensive until I realized that the people who make these statements are jealous or envious of the time and money my parents were able to spend on me." (Bernice Eiduson, speaking at the 1976 American Psychological Association session on the only child, wondered, "Is there something Calvinist around us that gives excuse for this self-righteousness? that disapproves of lavishness?")

Perhaps the word "spoiled" is used reflexively when another word, used *reflectively*, would be called for. Marguerite Krebs tells the story of a ready-to-disapprove pediatrician who examined a gurgling, vocal four-month-old whose professional mother had made it clear this baby was to be an only. "My, this one sounds spoiled," the pediatrician remarked nonchalantly. "Excuse me, no," the mother replied. "The word you want is *verbal.*"

A Miami child psychiatrist adds, " 'Spoiled' obviously has no literal meaning as a behavior or personality description. It applies to eggs, not people. It's usually supposed to mean 'materially indulged' or 'insistent upon having one's way.' To my observation, you can see such tendencies in only children. But I've seen them more frequently in the only girl in a large family of boys, the only male in a large family of females, or in last-borns of either sex. These are *not* just only-child traits."

Other counselors add that noticeably indulged birth situations within the family constellation include: a long-awaited child of either sex; a last-born greatly separated by years from his older siblings. "If you are looking for a birth order predisposed to 'spoiling,' " recommends Joyce Halstedt, "look for a last-born male who has two or more older sisters!"

The story of just such a last-born male is told in a recent political biography. A certain politician from a western state continually relied on his older sisters for help "with little things." One would help him shop for clothes during a congressional recess, another would do his laundry. One time a neighbor dropped in and found two sisters standing behind their brother, who stood facing a mirror. One by one, they took his ties, draped them around his neck and knotted them. He then carefully loosened each one and took it off so that when he returned to Washington he would not have to tie them himself. (Since this is precisely the sort of "spoiling" commonly associated with an only child, it might bear repeating that this politician in question *had four siblings!*)

It is also worth mentioning that when the above anecdote was read by an acquaintance of mine, a doctoral candidate in psychology, his response was, "Well, that's an only-child syndrome if I ever saw one." It was in just that casual a manner that I became aware of the most devastating evidence of prejudice of all: When psychologists and psychiatrists use the term "only-child syndrome" they are *not necessarily speaking* of a person with no siblings. They're just describing anyone who is overindulged or unsharing. Thus the only-child stereotype, if rid from psychology in the research department, is still "cemented in" to the very psychological lexicon!

Presumed loneliness and imagined lack of adjustment are also widely recalled by only children:

My mother's friends visited often and cluck-clucked because I didn't have someone to play with. Guess I heard this once a week between ages six and eight. Might have heard it oftener but I was usually out playing with somebody.

My high school was a rather advanced and experimental one—a lab high school on a college campus. My classes benefited from newest equipment, teaching and testing techniques, and, supposedly, counseling. At the beginning of tenth grade, we all saw a counselor. Mine said to me, "You are an only child. You can expect difficulty in relating to classmates. But I hope you will try very hard to make friends.' This seemed odd to me, as it was only the third day of school and I already had pals. I decided to seek out a few other only children who had that same counselor. We had all gotten the same treatment. We laughed about it, saying,

"Well, what does she know?" We felt we knew ourselves better than she did. But I wish we had confronted her with our feelings, then and there, because I've often wondered just how many other only children she greeted with that same speech.

Parents of only children, as well as the children themselves, face disapproval—and in fact more naked disapproval and direct criticism. True, the children can easily face hurtful epithets. But there is often a degree of ambiguity ("No brothers and sisters? Oh, I see . . .") which the child *may* manage not to understand but which the adult cannot help but recognize. Then, too, nobody could logically say to an only child, "How *dare* you have no brothers or sisters," but people *can* and often do say to the *parent* of an only such things as, "How *dare* you deprive your child . . ." etc.

A higher percentage of parents of only children than of only children themselves gave examples of social criticism. Of over two hundred questionnaires completed by parents of onlies, just *three* said they had never experienced criticism of their decision. And of these three, one works for Zero Population Growth and another indicated a similarly rarefied social environment by penciling in the margin of the questionnaire, "Are you kidding? I live in Berkeley."

Yet other parents of onlies who live and work in what could be considered liberal personal, social, or work environments regularly reported criticism. Said one highly placed professional woman, "My son's school claims there is no problem with only children, yet his teacher always makes a point to say something like, 'You'd never know he was an only.'"

Asked to indicate whether they felt social prejudice against one-child families to be "negligible," "slight," "moderate," "severe," or "so severe as to threaten our resolve to have only one child," the two-hundred-plus parents of onlies gave responses which break down as follows:

Degree of prejudice perceived to be:	*Percentage of respondents:*
Negligible	Less than 1%
Slight	3%
Moderate	40%
Severe	41%
So severe as to threaten our decision to have 1 child	17%

If the two "Severe Prejudice Perceived" categories are added together, the results might be compared to those of an earlier study by Erwin S. Solomon, *et al.*, "Social and Psychological Factors Affecting Fertility," published in the *Milbank Memorial Fund Quarterly,* in which 68 percent of mothers of only children and 49 percent of fathers of only children stated perceptions of "very much" social pressure to have a second child in order to avoid having an only child.

Excluding the "Gee, it's a shame" type of remarks built on the "There must be a medical problem" presumption, the great majority of prejudicial remarks reported by parents of onlies centered (again!) on selfishness, this time with a double edge: Not only were their only children sure to be selfish, but it is certainly selfish of the parents to create a family situation in which the child's selfishness is sure to occur!

Two Ohio couples kept track of criticisms they received during the week after they got their questionnaires. The Number 1 critical comment in both cases was "selfish."

Comments noted by 1st couple (child is 6 years old):
"You are being too *selfish* in your desire for freedom" (3 times)
"Child will be *selfish*" (6 times)
"You are being *selfish* in not giving families more grandchildren" (twice)
"Child will be lonely" (twice)
"More children will give you better care in old age" (once)
"Family will be happier" (once)
"Child needs to learn to share" (once)
"Child needs to learn to fight" (once)

Comments noted by 2nd couple (child is 4 1/2 years old):
"It's *selfish* of you (said to wife) to want to go back to your job" (twice)
"Peter will grow up to be *selfish*" (3 times)
"I know a man who grew up as an only who is so *selfish* he doesn't want *any* kids" (once)
"Just think of how nice it would be for Peter to have a brother" (once)
"You don't want to spoil him, do you?" (once)
"You're such good parents you should have more kids, lots more" (once)

Even college students, who might be presumed to be more liberal and open-minded on any aspect of life-style or family style, seem to have strong negative preconceptions about only children.

In a recent study at Wake Forest University, Bepi Pinner and Vaida Thompson asked college students to describe what they thought only children were like on a checklist of adjectives. Adjectives most often chosen: self-centered, attention-seeking, unhealthy, dependent, temperamental, anxious, unhappy.

A similar study by Sharryl Hawke and David Knox asked university students to complete the statement "An only child is _____." Only 11 of 133 responses described the only child favorably. The others suggested the by now unsurprising variety of personal handicaps.

Yet another essay with this projective technique was designed by Dr. David Martin and Linda Bumgardner of Nashville, Tennessee, in which 160 undergraduates were asked to:

1. Circle the words you believe descriptive of *the only child:*

neurotic	intelligent	hostile	sociable
immature	affectionate	honest	industrious
friendly	calm	lonely	stubborn
close to parents	happy	moral	conceited
ambitious	responsible	insecure	sickly
disobedient	strong	selfish	dependable

2. Circle the words you believe describe a *child from a large family:*

neurotic	intelligent	hostile	sociable
immature	affectionate	honest	industrious
friendly	calm	lonely	stubborn
close to parents	happy	moral	conceited
ambitious	responsible	insecure	sickly
disobedient	strong	selfish	dependable

It should come as no shock that Martin and Bumgardner found that "The only child was seen as immature, lonely, insecure, conceited, and selfish.

"By contrast, the child from a large family was seen as friendly, ambitious, affectionate, happy, responsible, sociable, and industrious," and received a more favorable rating on twenty-three of the twenty-four adjectives used in the study—the single exception seemed to grudgingly acknowledge that the only child might be more "intelligent."

One vital additional item on the Martin-Bumgardner questionnaire revealed that *not one* of the undergraduates expressed a desire to have just one child.

With such an aversion to the only child among a relatively elite educational group, the authors in fact wondered "if a term like 'onliest' should be coined to take its place along with 'racist,' 'sexist.' "

What is at work here, as friends and relatives and coworkers and neighbors confront the hapless one-child family, might once have been called folk wisdom, folk myth, or old wives' tales. It might seem more contemporary to coin a term such as *lay personality theory:* a significant phenomenon in America today.

The only trouble is that lay personality theory as applied to a supposed "only-child syndrome" is based on no solid gestalt. Its sources are diverse: literature and media stereotypes, outmoded and prejudicial professional opinions, rumor and assumption, and direct experience which may or may not be wisely perceived and interpreted. All these sources, of course, interact—and have for a long time.

Take a notable and critically timed example of the only child in literature.

Émile Zola's *Fécondité,* first published in 1899, paints a most unflattering portrait of "the adored only son." Coddled and overprotected, sturdy but always attended by doctors, capricious and tyrannical, the child is first pictured by Zola lying wearily on a sofa as his mother and physician stand near:

> The child had a stout appearance, a great resemblance to his father, the jawbone thicker. But he was pale, with limp eyelids, slight rings under the eyes. The mother, gazing at him with egoistic pride, kept the hand of her little son in hers. . . .[3]

The interest of this portrait lies partly in the contrast the author creates between the apparently sturdy physique of the child and his atony, or indolence. Later on, the boy's caprices, alimentary difficulties, and troubles in relating to other children are emphasized.

As pointed out by French sociologist Jean-Pierre Almodovar, Zola's portrait here is not far removed from two later "professional" assessments of only children:

> The only child, in spite of his appearance, is a handicapped child at the outset, who does not have the same chances for adjustment and success as others.
>
> *(Dictionnaire de Psycho-pedagogie)*

> The only child will be fragile, capricious, timid, tyrannical with his family, indolent. He will have some difficulties in adjusting to his comrades and integrating himself into a group. *(Manuel de Psychiatrie Infantile)*

And the novel predates by a year the first supposedly "scientific" survey on only children, in which E.W. Bohannon claimed that only children have poor health, are selfish, and get to school late!

Using Bohannon's study as a reference, G. Stanley Hall asserted in 1930: *"Being an only child is a disease in itself."* And one can get some idea of the effect of Hall's negative opinion of only children when it is realized that *Hall trained thirty of the first fifty doctorates in psychology in the United States!*

Just how "scientific" Bohannon's study was was later widely questioned. He simply asked a group of teachers to describe an only child whom they had taught—and it's not assuming too much to imagine that the exceptional or troublesome students in any group might spring first to a teacher's mind, particularly in that day and age when discipline and orderliness were considered desirable in those being educated.

For that matter, though often referred to in glowing terms such as "the earliest great child psychologist" by anthologists, G. Stanley Hall himself was capable of some fairly bizarre thinking. He founded the first organization and national magazine for child study, and published the first book on the psychology of adolescence, but the mantle of leadership did not keep him from such flights of fancy as suggesting, in his "theory of recapitulation," that a child passes through stages of development comparable to all those experienced over the *general social history of humankind,* i.e., in the child's play we see a hunting period, a food-gathering phase, a building era, etc.

No one seemed to think at the time that this was silly— perhaps in part because Hall's views on the only child seemed forecast by a man of great reputation for literary insight.

Of course it is not so simple as a chain reaction that began with Zola—but Zola's novel did appear in Europe late in his career, when, his reputation established, everything he wrote was widely read *and* just at the time psychology was developing as a science on the European continent.

Then, too, French academics have been noted for viewing literature as hardly separate from life. In fact, until the early 1940s it was possible in virtually all French universities to receive a doctorate in psychology as a result of analyzing literary characters rather than real persons!

It is certainly in order to question whether Émile Zola had a creative motive other than literary truth in developing his characters in *Fécondité,* for Zola was known as an ardent social reformer and socialist as well as a writer. Disapproving of capitalism, fearing industrialism—thinking that "differential fertility" according to class perpetuated both—recognizing that the rich had relatively low fertility and at times only children and thus passed on their wealth in great blocks, might not Zola have had a vested interest in a negative portrait of the only child?

In fact, later in his novel he rather gives this game away:

> On the one hand, the rich with an only son, had the obstinacy to constantly produce no increase (in social population) but only in wealth.

Just to make sure his point will not be lost (*Fécondité* cannot be called one of this writer's subtler novels), Zola describes not one one-child family but many: some wealthy, some crassly ambitious but not yet wealthy, but all pathogenic compared to the vigorous family of the hero who lives on a farm with *thirteen* healthy and enviable children.

At almost exactly the same moment, Henry James was presenting his readers, on both sides of the Atlantic, with a lonely only child in a portrait of far more psychological subtlety: *What Maisie Knew*. While literary prejudice against the only child easily calls for extensive treatment as a subject in itself, a few more examples readily come to mind within this same period: the "lonely onlies" such as orphans Jane Eyre and David Copperfield, Esther of *Bleak House* and Eppie in *Silas Marner* (as well as the narrator and his daughter in *Swann's Way* and Pearl in *The Scarlet Letter*); the "antisocial onlies" Huck Finn and Tom Sawyer, only slightly more renegade than picaresque but later misogynistically refined to pure malevolence in *Lolita* and *The Bad Seed;* the "selfish onlies" of turn-of-the-century children's literature: *The Little Princess* and her "rich petting father" in 1905; the sickly Carol Bird in *The Birds' Christmas Carol,* who as an only daughter gazes longingly at the large family next door, the Rugglesbys, in the same year that the foppish and vaguely ridiculous *Little Lord Fauntleroy* was presented to young readers.

With eerie likeness, Martin and Bumgardner's students seem to echo Zola's pronatalist portrayal, even using many of the same words the novelist employed: the child from a large family was seen as affectionate, happy, healthy, sociable, industrious . . .

It seems a long leap, in time and imagination, from Medan, France, where Zola wrote *Fécondité,* to a college in Nashville, Tennessee, where the 160 students tested by Martin and Bumgardner echoed Zola's agrarian-socialist ideals by sorting adjectives on checklists—assigning children from large families traits of happiness and vigor, and to only children the bleakest of personal characteristics.

A long leap—and not a simple one. Zola did not *create* Bohannon, Bohannon did not will Stanley Hall into being,

Hall did not then consciously indoctrinate early psychologists in some "domino theory of the mind."

When the best-known of Viennese psychiatrists stated, "The only child is a complete failure," and an early and influential book in the area of child guidance concluded, "The only child is greatly handicapped," who is to say that either the psychiatrist or the child-guidance expert had ever read Zola?

Yet influence can be indirect as well as obvious, and there is even today to the analyst of reproductive issues (e.g., abortion) an internecine relationship between experts' stands on issues and public opinion; between literature and media image, and components of popular psychology. (No doubt the 1972 Supreme Court had read the 1971 Gallup Poll; the creators of *Maude* had heard of Garrett Hardin and NOW.)

Similarly, in the late nineteenth century, pronatalist thought was not confined to one novelist, nor even to one artistic genre. In the visual arts, for instance, Greuze initiated a genre of *Beloved Mother* and *Beloved Child* paintings which moved one contemporary critic to say "[These paintings] say to all men of feeling and sensibility: 'Keep your family comfortable; give your wife as many children as you can; and be assured of being happy at home.' "

Feminist art historian Carol Duncan in fact documents an energetic "campaign for motherhood" in the art and literature of Western Europe at this time, speculating that this campaign may have been precipitated by growing use of contraceptives among European women. Male public opinion vehemently condemned contraception; men felt threatened, for whatever social change might be wrought by control of fertility could not be foreseen. ("Sexual freedom for women? Unthinkable!" one imagines a panicked interior monologue.) Perhaps just such fears create all the *isms,* in this case *pronatalism,* with its disapproval of the only child.

Rousseau, Greuze, Fragonard, Zola, Bohannon, Stanley Hall—all could be seen to be part of it. The interweaving elements of art, literature, psychology created impressions so strong and so persistent that they proved capable of withstanding, later, more empirical viewpoints. By 1930, a powerful pronatalist mythology had been created, as the impact of a few opinion leaders of the day reached the public via popular media and took root within both scientific and artistic disciplines.[4]

Thus, in some loose sense, Zola's hero with thirteen children *did* beget the Rugglesbys, whose children were the Gilbreaths, and whose grandchildren are the Waltons.

Paralleling the extravagances of the literary and media leaders and forgetting the cooler dispassionate prose supposed to characterize the scholar, early family scientists informed us that only children have "boundless egotism," "tyrannize over their friends," "will suffer no other gods before them." "In them, nervous manifestations thrive."[5] Having cited these in his book *Your Nervous Child,* Wexberg himself then concludes, "Only children are particularly imperiled under all circumstances."

Long after IQ means and achievement levels of only children were beginning to be noticeable, the prestigious *Encyclopedia of Child Care and Guidance* (1954) advised parents that "the only child need not be thought of as a complete tragedy." (The implication is fairly obvious!) A few years later, in 1959, *Complete Child Care in Body and Mind* stated, "The only child is selfish, overprotected, and immature." And an up-to-the-minute AMA book on children, *Growing Pains,* states categorically, "the only child is a lonely child."

To what can such opinions be attributed except to the persistence of myth? Indeed, the myth appears not only to have persisted but to have developed a few new strains suited to the contemporary literary soils of subtlety or sensationalism.

In what seems prejudice so subtle as to almost be self-parody, a 1975 women's magazine story begins:

> Show me a twenty-eight-year-old only child and I'll show you someone who has to sleep with his bed facing north, someone who will not answer the phone even if he is sitting next to it because he's sure it won't be for him, someone who wants me to make the kind of coffee you grind yourself in a little machine and then drip hot water over in another little machine. Show me an only child and I'll show you someone who owns seven raincoats.[6]

This contrasts in style with the bizarre May 1976 *Midnight* story "The Baby She Can Never Kiss." The infant told of in this *Midnight* special has many medical difficulties which seem insurmountable: a rare immunity deficiency, inevitable mental regression, and an intolerance to the touch of another human being so total that a kiss could be fatal. This is bleak enough, but what is infant Jennifer's worst problem? *"Being an only child will handicap Jennifer throughout her life,"* reporter Bernard Gould concludes.[7]

The effect of such stuff is reflected in a few stark statistics: while 3 of the 160 undergraduates in the Martin-Bumgardner study already referred to planned to have no children, *not one* stated a desire to have an only child; a 1970 Gallup

Poll revealed that 71 percent of a cross-section of Americans felt being an only child was a disadvantage—*up* from the 1950 Gallup figure of 60 percent.

Contemporary prejudice against the one-child family falls roughly into three categories:

1. Direct statement of negative attitudes
2. Indirect indication of internalized negative attitudes
3. Partial or complete omission of only children from a particular authority's scope of sight or frame of reference

Examples just cited are clearly of the first type—as is a 1971 *Life* magazine article in which one Dr. Albert Rosenfeld unabashedly confesses, "I have always liked to keep track of those figures of history who were the products of oversized families—Benjamin Franklin, for one, was the 15th of 17—and to point to the vigor and achievements of prolific contemporary clans like the Rockefellers and the Kennedys and the Buckleys. Besides, doesn't everyone know," he continues, "that lonely only children nearly always turn out to be full of troubles? How come it's suddenly so chic and wholesome to be practically alone in the house?" (He is being serious.)

More subtle and more interesting prejudice is shown in the value system revealed that same year by Dr. Gilbert Kliman, founder and director of the Center for Preventive Psychiatry, who contended in an interview, "Any child in any family is in danger of at least two kinds of mental illness. One is neurosis, imposed on a child by overattention—a greater hazard therefore in a small family. The other is *psychosis or a criminally inclined personality*,[8] a deprivation disease due to *lack* of parental attention—hence more likely in a large family." *Yet* Kliman opines, simplistically, "A large family is insurance against loneliness."

Norma E. Cutts and Nicholas Moseley, after taking a largely innovative view of the only child in their 1954 book of that title, summarized their research findings as follows:

> Our case histories indicate that the great majority of only children grow up to be well-adjusted adults. They have jobs that they like. They are happily married. They are taking an active part in the social life of their communities and bearing their fair share of public duties. These are signs of a healthy personality.

Nonetheless, the authors oddly opine at the end of their book,

> We feel that, if circumstances are favorable, it is a mistake to limit a family to one child. We think being an Only is hard on a child. We think parents who love each other and like children are missing a great deal in life if they have only one child. We think that parents who are deliberately limiting themselves to a single child should review their reasons with open minds.

Perhaps the above quotations reflect the difference between intellect and emotion, observation and feeling: the difference between "Our case histories indicate . . ." and yet "We feel . . . we think . . ." Any other interpretation of this disparity is difficult, for Cutts and Moseley present, throughout *The Only Child, no reasons* for thinking or feeling "it is a mistake to limit a family to one child."

Cutts and Moseley may have been trying to end stereotypical thinking about onlies, but their own conditioning as well as the "expert" opinions of those authorities they interviewed may have handicapped them. For example, leading obstetricians they asked replied uniformly that "almost never" did they feel a difficult first pregnancy should deter a woman from trying to have a second child; of one patient who absolutely could not attempt a second pregnancy a doctor's pronatalist bias is evident when he reports that her first delivery was "luckily twins."

A generation passed before another major book on the only child appeared, yet pediatrician Murray Kappelman's 1975 book, *Raising the Only Child,* reveals attitudes that have improved barely, if at all, toward the one-child family.

Statements throughout the book such as "The only child *can* be as normal and contented as any other kid on the block," "The only child *need not* feel like a social reject," and "Being an only child *need not* cause an unhappy life" seem to be damning with faint praise, to say the least.

Further, Kappelman's overattention to hazards of onliness—dependency, rebellion, loneliness, fantasies, recurring insecurities—is merely anecdotal, untempered by even a mention of more than twenty survey reports on such qualities of only children gathered in 1974 by the Department of Health, Education, and Welfare in a large volume that should have been easily accessible to him!

Spuriously anecdotal too seem a few of his stories of autocratic only children unparalleled anywhere:

> Arriving for a house call one cold December evening I was about to ring the doorbell, when the high-pitched voice of a five-year-old boy rang out through the closed front door: "Mommy, get me the comic book." "Daddy, I want a coke." As I stood there in the cold, listening, new commands were

issued in rapid succession. Finally, I rang the bell. A frenzied, flushed father opened the door. He smiled wanly and directed me toward the bedroom of his only son, who was sitting up majestically in bed surrounded by toys, comic books, candy, food, and other temporarily discarded delights. The child viewed me with suspicion; I had intruded upon his castle.

When Kappelman speaks affectionately and admiringly of the "experience and knowledge" that seem to come naturally to parents of large broods, he is being nostalgic, not scientific. When he describes his wife's panic at fixing her first baby's first formula and parenthetically mentions "Joan was an only child" in apparent explanation of her confusion, he is being gratuitous. And when he makes such contentions as "Summers can be devastating for the only child," he is missing the point. (Summers can be devastating for *any* child who loves school, its routines, its social life, its learning.)

Nancy Cox of the Maryland Commission on the Status of Women commented in a review of *Raising the Only Child,* "As the parent of one child by choice, I was eager for this book. But the hazards of my situation were so overwhelmingly presented chapter after chapter that I was nearly horrified. How many readers, I wondered, would receive the idea that the best solution to their situation would be to have another child? The advantages Dr. Kappelman finally presents are too few, and come too late in the book. For some, they won't be enough."

The tradition of negative attitudes toward only children was continued a year later in Lucille Forer's *The Birth Order Factor.* A description of only child Madeline is as fair an example as any of a dozen that might be chosen to reveal Dr. Forer's internalized attitudes:

> Madeline, an only child, was a young married woman who sought counseling because she found it difficult adjusting to her husband and coping with two small children. Madeline was immature. Her parents had never given her a chance to grow up, and her mother had done everything for her. As we talked *I noticed signs of loneliness and protective isolation, which so often characterize the only child* [emphasis mine].

Now, in normal conversation, just how does one reveal signs of loneliness and protective isolation? an inquisitive reader might wonder.

Perhaps part of the problem with Kappelman and Forer is that they function in therapeutic situations. Forer, a clinical psychologist, comes into professional contact only with individuals who have problems anyway; Kappelman, a pediatrician, is an easy recipient for years of stories of problems which parents of only children have mentioned when they visit his office, but were there no parents of only children who calmly brought their child in for an annual checkup, chatted about, say, the weather rather than their child's psychological problems—*then walked out?*

One invariably feels that there is an entire world of healthily functioning only children which two contemporary books have managed largely to ignore.

Ignoring the only child entirely may be the most devastating prejudicial device of all. Child developmentalists tell us that the most irreparable damage done to any young person results not from beating or other sorts of physical abuse but from behaving—in the presence of the child—as though the child just isn't there!

Minority groups came recently to see the importance of recognition by the media, for the implicit meaning of *lack* of recognition carries the same scary message a six-year-old receives when Mom or Dad ignores him: *You do not exist.*

In just the same way, when a life-style option is ignored by professional writings, lay opinions, and the media, the option to some extent is closed if not made entirely nonexistent. Consider as typical a passage from a 1976 book *Now That You've Had Your Baby:*

> There are important physical reasons for spacing your children . . . planned spacing gives your body a chance to regain its strength and return to a normal state . . . so that no matter how you feel about birth control socially or philosophically, you should for health reasons not immediately become pregnant again.[9]

However varied may be their readers' attitudes toward birth control (and the authors seem to suspect more reluctance than in fact exists), the authors' own feelings about *too much* birth control are clear! To deduce that they are skittish about such commonplace ideas as tubal ligation after the first child (up 56 percent in the last two years) or such suggestions as the *possibility* of "stopping at one" would be an overstatement. Such ideas are just not in their world. And, they are typical.

Eight of the ten top-selling works on child raising of the sixties and seventies fail entirely to mention the only child and contain instead strong presumptions of repeated reproduction: "*When* the second baby is brought home . . ." (Olshaker, *The Child As a Work of Art*); "Treat the *children* in your family as individuals . . ." (Salk, Kramer, *How to Raise a Human Being*); "How should we care for our *children?*" (Dodson, *How to Parent*); "Can you love all your *children* equally?" (Spock, *Problems of Parents*); "Parents should not be sucked into their *children's* sibling conflicts," (Gordon, *P.E.T.*) are examples (emphasis mine). *The Modern Parents Guide to Baby and Child Care* (1973); *Black Child Care* (1975); and *Whole Child, Whole Parent* (1975) also fail to recognize the only child.

Similarly, "Why have a pap test? Think of your *children,*" urges an American Cancer Society ad; "What do you do in case of a nuclear accident? Kiss your *children* good-bye," warns an antinuclear proliferation poster.

One speaks constantly of having *children* (or even of *not* having *children*), while to speak of children in the singular is a relative rarity.

The earliest birth-order researcher, Sir Francis Galton, looked at hundreds of outstanding English men of science and found that first-born and only children predominated —but he did not distinguish between the two groups.

Over the years since Galton's 1874 report, several dozen studies could be effortlessly cited in which birth-order researchers give not the barest hint that such a thing as an only child exists!

A 1964 report on National Merit Scholarship winners is as good an example as any. Examining 1,618 student finalists within this elite group, Robert C. Nichols of NMSC dutifully reported the percentage of *first-born* winners from two-child families (66 percent) and first-born winners from three-child families (52 percent) and from four-child and five-child and six-child families. (Always, the first-born predominated, with a downward stairstep progression as birth order rose; latter-borns are rarely present.) But

Nichols made no mention of only children—though it would be impossible to believe they were not represented in this group![10]

Following tradition, publishers of directories of distinguished individuals such as Marquis' *Who's Who* do not ask birth-order information on biographical questionnaires sent to listees.

A fascinating *McCall's* Gallup-commissioned survey showed one in ten American parents to be so disenchanted with their role that—given the choice again—*they would not have children.* Fascinating, but it might have been helpful and enlightening to know whether the *number of children* correlated in any way with the unhappiness of these parents. Gallup did not ask.[11] Nor did *Redbook* ask birth-order information in its survey of female sexuality published in 1975, nor did *Glamour* in a recent (1976) and very typical birth-order article ("Are You the Oldest, Youngest, or In-Between Child?") say anything about only children.

It seems fair to conclude that the only child has been subject to a "selective inattention" too great to be explained by accident, random error, or oversight. Surely the persistent avoidance by scholars and popular writers of such a pertinent birth-order aspect might *not* be purely accidental, but might instead result from one of several biases: a feeling that the subject is so simple that everyone knows all about it anyway . . . or so trivial and unimportant that no one need care . . . or so ugly that it is best left alone . . . or that it's just *not there.*

Does something about the one-child family still make a society that has embraced a half-dozen other nontraditional life-styles in as many years still generally uneasy? If so, why? Dr. Jacob Arlow in a closely related context speaks of envy, believing that "The widely prevalent notions about the only child as a special type of person who is neurotic, self-centered, unable to tolerate frustration, noncompetitive, demanding, and hypochondriacal may well arise from the envy and hostility felt by those individuals who are struggling with intense sibling rivalry."[12] An intriguing possibility but of course not a total explanation.

Certainly, not all literature is false, nor is all professional psychology stupid, nor are all lay and professional theoreticians of only-child psychology motivated by blind jealousy or "intense sibling rivalry." But certainly some element of envy may give root to the prejudice. How many of those of us who are not only children felt disadvantaged compared to those we knew who *were*, and found therefore the negative stereotypes of onlies very convenient to seize on so that we might feel better off, after all.

An additional and important possibility not considered thus far is suggested by Marguerite Krebs of Ann Arbor, Michigan. One reason for viewing only children negatively, she suggests, is that they may have been genuinely, generally disadvantaged at one time. "In past years, only children may have had their problems," she feels, *"not due* to their being only children, but due to their parents' reasons for having only one child."

For previous generations, "reasons" for having only children may not have been "reasons" in the sense of conscious planning, but more the result of unfortunate circumstance.

When infant mortality was high, a child might have become an *only* because all his brothers or sisters died. When genetics was little understood, a physically imperfect firstborn might have dictated a decision to have no later-borns.

Before birth control was reliable, an only child might have occurred as an accident to a couple who wanted to remain childless. Before divorce was common, severe estrangement between spouses might have meant no sexual union after early years of marriage and one child. It is easy to see how any of these "reasons" for the one-child family *could* have caused a troubled psychological profile for the only child.

But motivations for having only children today are, according to all evidence, generally healthy, altruistic, and caring. They reflect positive feelings about self, spouse, child, and life; desire for personal growth, depth of experience, development of child, concern for community. It is no longer justifiable, if it ever was, to meet the idea of an only child with an attitude of "Oh, too bad" or similar expressions of prejudice.

Some will find the label of "prejudice" applied to the one-child family faintly ridiculous. "Prejudice implies victimization," I've been told, "and only children are merely inconvenienced." I agree only with clause one.

Prejudice literally means "pre-judging" someone according to a class or category, not as an individual. That happens to only children. They are necessarily then made "victims" according to how their category is perceived. Granted, sometimes the *consequences* of prejudice are more severe than at other times. Most imagine victims of prejudice to be deprived in some serious or fundamental way: deprived of life, property, freedom of movement, or opportunity. But isn't a prejudice that can remove even one choice of *how you will live your life* equally serious? Isn't a mind-set that categorizes only children as problematic and different equally unfair?

I know of four cities in which parents of only children have formed informal groups that meet regularly to share both problems and mutual support. I can think of no more decisive indication that serious prejudice exists, and change is needed.

Right now, for the first time in many years, the one-child family is gaining popularity as a preferred family size. Of wives aged eighteen to twenty-four who expect to have one child, the percentage has almost doubled, from 6 percent in 1967 to 11 percent in 1975. A Youth Research Organization poll among high school and college-age young adults aged fourteen to twenty-five also reflects a near-doubling, but in a much shorter time: moving from 6 percent in 1972 to 10 percent in 1974.

But *preferred* family size is not always *actual* family size, and it may not be for these young adults if they move from a tolerant and liberal academic atmosphere out into jobs and neighborhoods where their desire to have an only child will face criticism and perhaps hostility. Indeed, perhaps the only way they can be assured that they *can* choose to have one child, if that's what they want, is to resolutely say an abrupt good-bye to a past of myth and prejudice against the only child.

Chapter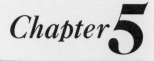

One Child: The
Pleasures and Problems

I went downstairs to the candy store below our apartment to
buy comic books. Some kids from the neighborhood were
sitting at the table in the back. I walked over to them. "Hi."
They were looking at cards with pictures on them. I watched
for a while. "What're those?"

One of them looked up. "You kiddin'?" I didn't answer.
"Boy, anyone don't know what these is must be pretty
dumb."

"Well, it ain't dumb just 'cause I never saw somethin'
before!" I looked around the table hoping to find someone
who'd agree with me but they all just shook their heads like
I was too stupid to live. I was dying to walk away but I knew
if I said, "Well, so long," nobody'd answer.

"These're baseball cards, dopey! Where y'been all your
life?" The most any of them had was about a dozen. I had
a ten dollar bill in my pocket. The bubble gum the cards
came in was a penny apiece. I bought a hundred of them.

They all stopped talking. I played it big, pulling the cards
out of the packages, piling them into one tall stack. The boy
who'd first called me dumb came over and looked eagerly at
my cards. "Y'wanta trade?"

"Sure. Whattya wanta trade?"

He picked out three. "I'll take these."

"Okay, but what'll you give me for 'em?" I didn't care but I didn't want to look dumb again. He handed me three of his cards and I looked at them as if I knew one from the other.

"Fair 'nuff?" he asked. I nodded. He shouted, "Trade's off 'n no trades back!" and all the other kids burst out laughing. He grinned. "Boy, you really are dumb. Anybody who'd give up a Babe Ruth or a Lou Gehrig for less'n five cards—boy, that's the dumbest thing I ever saw."[1]

Sammy Davis, Jr., remembers that incident from the time he was seven years old. Though his childhood was atypical in many ways other than onliness, the only child is often thought to be unsocialized—in short, "out of it."

To say, however, that a child is "out of it" is senseless without wondering, "out of *what?*" To some extent, perhaps as an outgrowth of creative pastimes or habits of autonomy, an only child may be "out of" the usual patterns of conformity. Often this is not true; sometimes it is. Sometimes *when* it is, there are adjustments that are quickly learned, as shifts are made from social to private situations. (One parent commented, "Jimmy speaks two languages. Kid and Adult.") Once in a while, *if* a sense of apartness is at all due to loneliness, an only child will sense this—and look for other only children!

One New York woman remembers when her only son was in kindergarten he talked for several days about a chart that he was making, promising to show it to her at the end of the week. When it was completed, it had sixteen lines with the names of the sixteen children in his kindergarten class and a number in a box after each name. Five-year-old Larry had conducted his first survey. He had asked each of his new classmates how many brothers or sisters they had in order to locate the one other child *who had none!*

But according to most observers, a sense of feeling apart or different has less to do with onliness than with other factors. "An only child is likely not to know what's going on if he is out of his age group; if he has just been introduced to a new school or a new neighborhood," says Marguerite Krebs. "But the same would be true of *any* child, with or without siblings. Parents just have to do a bit of 'cueing-in,' or create situations where other children can do this."

It *is* necessary to plan for playmates.

Children vitally need to learn to measure themselves against other children, experience the trial and error of initiating friendships. In fact *even before* children could be expected to "learn" very much by means of direct interaction, the mere presence of another child the same age is a good idea. "Three-year-olds play side by side, not *with* each other," one day-care supervisor observed. "It might look like they're oblivious to one another, so it might seem pointless to arrange to bring them together. But they're really learning by observing, watching. They're more aware of the other children, other styles of play, than they seem to be!"

Later, the importance of socialization increases.

Not many only children faced Tracy's situation of living in a neighborhood with virtually no children (teenagers didn't count, she recalls) when she was eight years old. Then, "I'll never forget that day. Mom and I were sitting on the front porch when *they* came—our new neighbors. I saw there was a girl my own age. *A girl my own age!* It was my earliest recollection of kids my own age nearby. I walked right over. Not much that I've been through in the twenty years since then matches the happiness I felt at that moment."

But that *was* twenty years ago and in an unusually isolated exurb. In most communities, finding age-group playmates will not be a problem. There are playgrounds; professionally staffed private day-care centers; parent-operated cooperatives that can be learned about (even in a new neighborhood) given a few hours on the telephone; and an increasing number of feminist-, "Y"-, and church-sponsored child-care groups. For that matter, it is a rare parent who has not thought ahead to the needs of a child and moved out of the Adults Only units of an apartment complex well in advance of the child's need for peers.

A Boston reporter found that while most parents-of-one were aware of planning for playmates more actively than if there were brothers and sisters around they were also sensitive to an only child's enjoyment of privacy. One Milton, Massachusetts, woman contributed the thought that a balance between a child's "society" and "self" was needed: "After she's come home from school or has been playing with friends, Joelie is delighted to have quiet private time. She's happy with it." And writer Jane O'Reilly mentions with approval her thirteen-year-old son's freedom from "compulsive gregariousness": "Ian would rather be home than many other places," she explains.

If only children seem to fit into their groups with somewhat less ease than other children, the appropriate analysis (Are they exercising autonomy or experiencing rejection?) and response on the part of the parents is vital, of course. "Only children do come out well in achievement," said one teacher, "and although they're not always 'tops' in everything, they're often very good at everything. . . . Depending upon what sort of achievement values surround them in their class, their excellence can be a potential sore spot with other children. It's the school's job—not just the parents' job—to be alert to such situations."

Not every parent is fortunate enough to have a school where teachers share that view. And often the child's first educational experience calls for careful monitoring by at least one parent. As to how "careful" such ideal monitoring should be, one mother was of the opinion that "it should stop just short of neuroticism."

"You have to know your child and how different he may be in energy or ability from other youngsters," explained another mother, Jeannette. "Chris, my son, is more independent than those his age and less likely, in spite of tremendous peer pressure to conform, to do things because everyone else does them. He does not cooperate in anything he feels is dumb. Thus he was kicked out of nursery school at age four for 'failure to respect the rest period,' and dismissed from a different and more advanced school one month later for not sitting still and learning the alphabet (he'd known it for years), and thus is on his way to being labeled *'uncooperative.'* "

The above mother's story is common, and sadly may have a great deal to do with continuing certain only-child stereotypes rather than dealing with their root causes. It's not unknown for a child (any child, not just an only) to begin to live up to the name or fit into the label if it seems to be the most significant identity component perceived by others around him.

Jeannette managed to solve her problem, and Chris's, with yet another change of nursery school: "If a child knows the alphabet, he's going to be out of place surrounded by children who don't," she correctly perceived. But what is vitally worth noting is that such was *her* perception, not the nursery school teacher's. Parents of only children may need to be more alert than most parents to the need for one or more changes in grade level during their child's school career.

It would be an oversimplification to assume only children are universally *the* top students, fastest learners, or generally the most outstanding students in their groups.

"Yet it does seem as though many only children are continually using the word 'only' in other ways," Marguerite Krebs has observed, "as in, 'I was the *only* one who knew all the spelling words,' 'I was the *only* one Joan's father said was well-behaved,' or 'I was the *only* one who finished two books during reading period.' " (One American couple who lived in England for a year even reported that their only son came home one day from his school in London and said, "I was the only one who knew how big a majority the Labor Party had in Parliament," adding, "and you know I think the teacher was mad because none of the English kids knew.")

It's certainly easy to understand that only children might be the "only" ones in a group to have certain advanced knowledge or abilities, even in political areas (they have no siblings to distract them with simpler matters when their parents discuss politics at dinner—the next day at some time they may quote a parent's opinion about a politician that is clearly beyond their years).

Such situations do not always cause problems, according to Krebs and other authorities, but it is up to the parents to assess whether or not problems may result. "If your only child's peers value associating with someone who knows a lot, you have no problem. If your child's associates don't comprehend it completely, they're apt to merely pretend they do in order to 'live up' to your only and thus you still have no problem—yet. But if your child must relate to a group generally envious of his/her superior knowledge, watch that the group members do not retaliate by refusing to play. *Then* you need to take action."

But again, the solution to such a problem does depend on appropriate action—*not deciding to acquire a sibling.* (After all, if your only child has established habits of achievement or superiority, he might well retain those habits even if a younger brother or sister were to be born. Though that advice should seem too obvious to bear mention, there is a story from the fifties, when female children were not "supposed" to be brilliant, told by counselor Delores Ann Hudson, then of Chicago, of a brilliant ten-year-old girl whose parents sought to "cure" her of her brilliance by having another child. The sad and rather predictable result? "The older girl kept right on being brilliant; her younger sister in her earliest years was given an extremely severe inferiority complex.")

Just as the presence of a sibling will not "cure" brilliance, neither will it "cause" sharing. Though parents are often urged to have a second child so that their first will "learn to share," that second child may be an expensive—and totally ineffective—"teacher."

Sharing represents moral, as opposed to intellectual, development, but according to Dr. Catherine Bateson, the two kinds of development have in common the need for specific, structured guidance: "You can't just assume that an only child is going to learn to live with other people. You have to construct something to make that possible."

Julie A. Cleare agrees, and further defines that "something to make [sharing] possible" as *gradual* and *minimal* exposure to other children. "If parents will keep in mind that 'maximum moral learning occurs with minimal socialization,' they'll be acting according to a fairly safe principle: certainly safer than the sudden and total 'immersion' socialization that arrives with a new sibling."

Though Cleare is not the only child psychologist to have observed that siblings often do not share, she offers an explanation more succinct than most: "Nothing about siblings automatically teaches sharing. Adults have to teach it."

In fact, can the presence of siblings *retard* tendency to share? Not only do many child-development authorities suggest this possibility, that experience is poignantly affirmed by a number of "almost-only" children:

"I was very sharing and giving until I was eight years old," recalls Brad. "I had figured out that sharing very seldom resulted in loss, and felt good even if it didn't bring a this-for-that benefit. The arrival of a step-brother my own age taught me differently. Shared items were broken or lost. I began to hide everything. I entered a period of stinginess that lasted well into high school. Then I thought I had gotten over my hoarding impulse but when I walked into my first college dorm room I caught myself glancing around trying to identify 'hiding places.' " Brad's experience is similar to those recounted by others who had full siblings rather than stepsiblings—perhaps even much less intense for lack of a years-long *history* of competition for a parent's attention.

(An adult parallel might further reinforce the point. Isn't it easier for adults to share with associates of *our* choosing, whose level of responsibility in caring for our possessions we can personally assess, than to share fully with house guests who arrive unbidden for an indeterminate stay?)

Given the importance attached to learning to share, it is surprising to find little specific advice for parents. ("The books just say 'Teach your child to share,'" complained one mother. "They don't say *how.*") Cleare advises flexibility, lack of insistence.

"Give opportunity but don't force. For instance, don't expect more than one half to one hour of socializing or sharing from a two-and-a-half-year-old. And don't assume you've failed if, after sharing a favorite toy for a while, your young child wants it back. Let him take it back. Then he'll feel more secure about sharing it again another time."

Krebs thinks it valuable if parents teach an only child to share with *them,* ("Even if you don't *want* half the candy bar, take it!") and oversee situations with other children where sharing is a possibility.

"You'll generally see the sharing happen naturally," she advises parents of onlies, *"more* easily in an only child than in one with a brother or sister. The only child learns that sharing *earns* pleasant feelings and rewards. It earns friends. A brother or sister's presence, however, doesn't need to be *earned:* a child can be unsharing and selfish and the brother or sister will still, inevitably, be around."

It has been known to happen that an extremely canny only child will not merely be unsharing but will use his onliness as an excuse for material aggrandizement. "I think you owe me a new bicycle," a nine-year-old girl is reported to have said slyly to her parents. "After all, shouldn't I have some compensation for not having any brothers or sisters?" Krebs, who heard that story through a fellow counselor, said that though the parents' specific response was not put on record, their quick decision had been to "nip this sort of [bribery] in the bud." There was no new bike.

Of course neither materialism nor any other exercise of ego is the exclusive province of the only. "I worry because he hears his name constantly mentioned on the phone. Will this make him self-centered?" is a common concern. But it applies as easily to an elder child, a younger child, a brighter child (even a favorite child) as well as to an only. It just seems that parents of only children worry more about such things.

"Is my child spoiled, or on his way to becoming spoiled?" asked Annette. "He's less than a year old but already seems to have a grasping attitude toward his play-things and does not want to give them up."

"Is our only son too self-centered?" inquired Mr. and Mrs. J., Detroit parents. "He is in first grade, and unless we ask specific questions about classmates or teachers talks almost exclusively about himself."

Relax a little, say most experts.

Charlotte and Karl Buhler in their studies of infants found that babies nine to twelve months of age generally object to giving up toys. They found this true of *all* infants, not just onlies.

Similarly, the famous child-development specialist Jean Piaget observed that the thinking of children under eight years old will normally be somewhat self-centered. And he observed this in *all* children, not just onlies.

Perhaps it's because pediatricians and counselors *hear* such worries voiced most often by parents of onlies that they are lead to the illusion that self-centeredness is some-how endemic to the situation of the only. "I think it's just that parents of one child are watching more closely," comments Cleare, adding that within very wide limits this monitoring is a healthy and positive practice.

"Monitoring" can of course turn into *hovering*. Some parents may be too protective, others may focus too many of their own ambitions on their child. It's even possible to encounter a complaint from an only child of having been "loved too much." If parental focus becomes burdensome, the child is pressured—perhaps to return an undue amount of affection, perhaps to achieve honors beyond his ability or desire.

Romain Gary describes such pressures with particular impact in his memoir, *Promise at Dawn*. Once, he recalls, after a particularly clumsy dancing lesson, his mother cried "Nijinski, Nijinski! You are going to be a second Nijinski— I know what I am talking about." She spoke with equal loftiness of other achievements that would surely be his: "The time will come when your name will be inscribed in letters of gold. . . . You'll be a d'Annunzio, a Victor Hugo, a *Nobel Prize winner.*" (Several writers, including Michael A. Sperber, have adopted the term "Nobel Prize syndrome" to describe achievement patterns among only children whether or not prompted by such ambitious parental attitudes.) Gary concludes, "It is wrong to have been loved so much."

Most authorities would reject not only Gary's analysis of the situation but would dismiss the very idea that there *can* be such a thing as "too much love" and insist instead on some very precise semantic distinctions. They would prefer to say that there can be too much possessiveness . . . too much attention . . . too much exclusivity . . . too much identity-investment . . . even too much *display* of love. But whether or not an excess of "love" is technically possible, a certain abundance can surely be *perceived* as "excessive" by the unfortunate children on the receiving end of it! When there is only one child, the lens of the parental microscope—the focus of the parental ambition—can overwhelm.

The problem can be exacerbated (as indeed in the case of Gary and his mother, Madame Kacew) when there is not only an only child, but an *only parent!*

Parent and child may begin to carry a "We are special friends" unity beyond healthy boundaries into a "Two against the world" isolation (even to the point of relating socially as a marital unit, the child becoming the parent's near-exclusive companion at parties, dinners out, etc.). Gary himself felt his too-close maternal ties due to the lack of a love interest in his mother's life: "If only my mother had had a husband or a lover!" he writes.

Fortunately, this particular phenomenon is rare. And it is one that rarely lasts very long, since it is easily recognized by friends if not the single parent himself or herself. "When I found myself asking my daughter's *permission* to go out on a date, I suddenly stopped in my tracks and said, 'Whoops . . . enough of this!' " reports Kay, a single, separated mother.

Not every instance, when it can be found, of parental overinvolvement is *maternal* overinvolvement (Mary Astor's *father* was just as guilty of it as Romain Gary's mother). Even a male professional, J.B. Watson, seemed to tacitly endorse the ambitious, "Nobel Prize" approach to childraising when he wrote, in 1925, "Give me a dozen healthy infants, well-informed, and my own specified environment for them, and I'll guarantee to take any one at random and train him to be anything I might select—doctor, lawyer, artist, merchant-chief." And it can be found less and less, according to reports.

"A mother of an only child today is almost sure to have professional or community interests, a career or outside life. Smothering maternalism is disappearing quickly," believes Marguerite Krebs. Another counselor, agreeing, adds, "When maternal overprotection is a concern, it's the mother of three or four you have to watch out for!"

Maternal overprotection today isn't even likely if mother and child live apart from the child's father, it seems. Gary may have attributed his mother's attentiveness to lack of a husband or lover, but lack of an outside *job* might be just as correct an analysis. Single mothers today automatically, it seems, project less focused ambition, have more balance among life roles—because they generally have to work!

The single-parent/single-child household is most apt to be threatened by any lingering hostilities between parents which fall upon the child—but here too the only child is by no means a special case. *Any* child can be expected to feel guilty, at first, when parents separate; it has to be explained to *every* child that he is not responsible. *Any* child needs help not only understanding the situation but explaining it to his friends. The presence of a sibling offers little practical support in most cases.

Many heads of single-child households view their situations with no small degree of optimism, pointing out many of the same advantages traditional one-child families enjoy: You *can* toss one in a car and go on a trip; you *can* take one to a neighbor's more easily if a sitter doesn't show up; you can even (in an emergency) take one along to an interview and leave him more gracefully in an outer office to read magazines quietly. And speaking of offices, one mother remarked, "If a business says they allow 'Kids in the Office' they really don't mean that in the plural!" Advantages of mobility, economic ease, unfragmented attention accrue almost as easily to one parent as to the traditional Mom-Dad duo.

If only children are not uniquely prone to problems—if, indeed, they show special development in so many ways—it should still be mentioned in passing that "special" does not quite mean *sainted.* I suppose the point is that the problems of only children are pretty much the problems of any other children. Faced with the task of growing into a world of larger, smarter people, all children at one time or another experience feelings of shyness or insecurity, loneliness or aimlessness, times of jealousy or fear, periods of temper, tendencies to disobey, and more.

And if only children *seem* to show differences in the nature or degree of their problems, should the differences between the onlies and the non-onlies be laid to the absence of siblings? Or to the *kind of parenting* present?

"If your only child is a problem child, you are out of luck," runs the argument. "But if you have more children, and one turns out wrong, you have extra chances to have another one turn out right."

Dr. E. James Lieberman zeros in on the weakness of that argument. Simply, a problem child likely results from poor parenting. "Thus, if a first child is maladjusted and parents then proceed to have other children, chances are good that the later children will be maladjusted too." (Further, a problem child presented with a baby brother or sister often becomes more of a problem than ever before!)

Several contributors to the anthology *Progress in Experi-*

mental Personality Research confirm this view: One writes, "When studies have found problems among only children, it is often seen that these same problems are experienced by first-borns and are not aided by the later addition of a brother or a sister."

"If you have a problem dog, you may want to get a second dog," commented one pediatrician, "if you have a problem plant, you may want a second plant for supplementary greenery. But if you have a problem child the solution is almost never a second child but a redesign of the attention and love you are presently giving the one you already have."

The *one* problem faced by single-child families exclusively seems to be social pressure and criticism. Being in the vanguard of an emerging life-style is seldom comfortable, but parents of onlies tend to feel their "vanguard" position totally lacking supportive troops as they must face hostility of an almost military nature.

Sometimes, when an "enemy strategy" is understood, the need for confrontation tactics disappears. Once in a while, what seems like a hostile question is just honest curiosity: *Why?* And many common criticisms can be answered simply, confidently, without embarrassment. "If my wife and I had enough savvy to *have* an only child," a husband told me, "it should by comparison be relatively simple to *explain* it!"

Though wit may not be as disarming as direct discourse, few parents of only children can resist its occasional deployment:

Criticism: Having a brother or sister is part of growing up.
Response: Nonsense. I grew up.

Criticism:	A little brother would give Johnny healthy conflict.
Response:	He already has a playground, a gym, and a Junior Health Club which offer boxing partners. And a career in the United States Marines is always possible.

Criticism:	I heard your Johnny say he wants a little brother.
Response:	We have also heard Johnny say he wants a new red wagon, and, if anything, we believe he has put more thought into wanting the new red wagon. We believe we may get him the red wagon.

Criticism:	Susie would have someone to be close to in adulthood if she had a sibling.
Response:	As an adult, I have one sibling I am close to and one I cannot stand. That makes the odds about even, and I'm afraid I'm not a gambler.

Criticism:	I've heard Susie say she'd like a brother or a sister.
Response:	That's only because she has not yet discovered she can beat up the Ruggles twins by herself.

And fifteen-year-old Scott LeCroy of Alabama wrote to *Psychology Today* (Aug. 1976) that "When someone questions my parents (both onlies) as to why they didn't have more kids, their answer is: 'We got it right the first time.' "

But such irreverence is best reserved for the really pesky. The elderly, well-meaning pediatrician who asks with genuine concern, "Hadn't you better have another? You don't want a genius on your hands, do you?" deserves better than, "Sure we do. We've skipped a generation"; and the heart-rending way your mother-in-law may have of introducing your child ("This is my *only* grandchild") calls more for compassion than comebacks.

Your reasons for having an only child, whatever they are, may be less challengeable than you think: A Kansas City couple discovered, "Though we are thought to be very well off, we honestly feel we cannot afford more than one. If we just say that, people accept it. Maybe they feel sorry for us, maybe they disbelieve us, I don't know. But they nod in approval and leave us alone after that."

The only child, too, will have his pressures. According to Krebs and others, it is essential to help equip your child to respond to the most common accusations: being selfish and spoiled. Children generally catch on quickly. When I asked one eight-year-old girl if she had ever been called spoiled, she said, "Yes, and my mother and I understand that. So when anyone says I am spoiled, I just smile at them. I don't want to give them any more ammunition."

Sometimes parents and their only child can find themselves responding to criticism jointly. Several times, I've been told of an only child coming to a parent's defense. "I hadn't even known Kenny had come into the room," the father of a six-year-old wrote, "but as a visitor got deep into the matter of how lonely Kenny must be, a small voice piped up and said, 'Mr. Johnson, I've got my dad to play with, and he's more interesting than a little kid.' "

Ironically, just such enviable vignettes of parent-child rapport spur a particular fear for what will happen to the only child when "the ties that bind" break finally. Many parents of one worry that their death will leave their child "alone in the world" or at least somewhat rootless: "When my husband and I die, our daughter will have no one with whom to reminisce about her childhood," one woman wrote, "and she is so close to us the shock to her might be unimaginably great."

"But death is never *not* a shock," mildly protested an adult only son at a rap group where that letter was anonymously read, "and I think the greatest wringing of hands when parents die is done by children who feel guilty for not treating their parents better."

Guilt is definitely one factor in grief, though not the only one, identified by those who have recently studied the phenomenon of death and dying. A stronger factor where only children are concerned seems to be that parents of one child by choice, being careful planners, tend to have their only child later. Thus, an only child *may* lose one or both parents earlier in maturity than, say, a larger brother-sister network born while parents were in their twenties. Encouragement might be taken from the statement made to this same rap group by a twenty-year-old teacher whose parents had died tragically (an auto accident had proved fatal for the wife; the grief-stricken husband succumbed to a heart attack en route to the hospital) within the past year. "I was always very close to my parents," Ursula told the group, "and felt very good about them. When I realized they were gone, without warning, so very suddenly, at first I was crushed. But I could honestly say I had no regrets about how I had treated them. I didn't go through the torment of thinking, 'How badly I treated them; if only I'd done thus-and-so.' It was a close and easy relationship . . . somehow I have to look at the parting in the same way."

A middle-aged Baltimore couple took a decidedly different view of the woman's letter. "The shock to our son of our death doesn't worry us in the least. Alone in the world? Nonsense! He'll do just fine. But we'd really like to make sure we don't burden him in old age should we live a long time and our health not be the best."

Probably that is a more common concern of parents of a single child, particularly given the tendency, well-described by Cutts and Mosely, of an only child to be devoted to aged parents to the point of sacrifice. It might seem odd that planning for old age should be an integral part of raising an only child, but such planning seems unarguably wise for *any* adult, parent of one, lots, or none. (Herbert Robbins remarks that "The high school student is urged to plan for college, the college student to plan for career and family. But once established in career and family there's no great prompting to plan for later years. This lack of planning can contribute significantly to later unhappiness—it may even be as major a factor in old age problems as the fanaticism of our 'youth culture.' ")

Marguerite Krebs feels it's important not just to begin to plan for postretirement while your only child is young but to fill your child in on your plans! Provide some education as to how responsibility between generations works, or doesn't.

A family I know provides an example of this. Husband and wife are both responsible for the care of their parents; the husband is an only child, the wife has two brothers and a sister, none of whom contribute in any way. There are occasional resentments, and there was one notable Christmastime explosion of bitterness by the wife when her brothers visited. None of this has been concealed from the couple's only son. Krebs approves of such candor. "If our own parents are not a burden," she says, "certainly we all know people who *are* too burdened. It's perfectly all right to point this out to your child and say, 'We will not be dependent on you like that.' "

Of course, when you tell your child, "We don't want to

be a burden," you should mean it, and not just be saying something that sounds noble while inwardly you nurse secret hopes for weekly visits. Cutts and Mosely, authors of an early book on *The Only Child,* have suggested some nononsense introspection: "If you are looking ahead and hoping to keep from being a burden on your child, it's a good idea to examine your attitude. Do you really think of the child as an individual and not just an extension of yourself? Do you agree that parents have no rights but many responsibilities? Are you expecting your child to lead an independent life?"

If your answer to that last question is an honest *Yes,* amends Krebs, you'll find yourself beginning in your child's teen years to use phrases like "When you move out . . ." and "When we move away . . ." and you'll use such phrases naturally and fairly often. And you'll mean them.

Sentimentalists may be skeptical, but many parents of one child actually look forward to living independently, with perhaps only the sort of contact with their only child that they might expect from a young friend they had known, or student they had housed or sponsored. Perhaps one father was right on target as he explained his own situation—his wife has died and his only son lives half a continent away: "As Chris grew older, our parent-child relationship changed to more of a friendship. Sometimes Chris was a fairly demanding friend, and I had to teach him that friendships are not to be exploited. Now, I have to remember that lesson myself. And I pretty much do. There are always other friends to be made, after all."

There is consensus on the generally easy transition to "empty nest" years on the part of parents who have had one child. Successful transition obviously has as its bottom line a sound emotional stability on the part of the parents. Parents of just one child tend to remain more whole, integrated personalities. They do not overinvest their identities in parenthood but rather keep their own interests and links to life in good repair. ("Empty nest?" said one. "We almost never noticed. The nest doesn't seem so empty if it has held *more* than chicks.")

Though this point has been addressed earlier, it is repeated here by way of introduction to a letter that might otherwise seem remarkable. It is not; indeed it is typical. This mother of one is clearly not sitting sadly waiting for a phone call or visit from the daughter she raised.

> Minneapolis, Minnesota
> July 10, 1976

Dear Hal and Nancy:

It was my sincere intention to write you weeks earlier—but alas other things crowded my life and cluttered up my desk. Sorry.

I have followed with interest your participation in so many worthwhile projects. I share your feelings in several areas—especially the eye bank, "death with dignity," and the view that if we do not care to inhale the smoke from others' cigarettes we should not be forced to do so.

When I look around me and see so many people of my age feeling poorly or unhappy I am profoundly grateful for my excellent health and overflowing social calendar. My only gripe is that there are not more than twenty-four hours in a day!

I cannot keep up with reading I want to do. Every day on my calendar has a luncheon, bridge date, church dinner, cocktail party, or something else on it. And my desk is always piled with unanswered letters. So many friends keep in touch, one way or another—letters, calls, visits (sometimes unannounced).

As I look out my window I see the tallest building in my town and was recently invited to lunch there. Have also taken numerous short trips the past 2 months—Quebec, Chicago, Montreal.

Of course I am following the candidates on television . . . but I haven't told you about my latest interest. I am a transcendental meditator! I had the instruction with friends and am so thankful that I had the wit and lack of prejudice to do this—it is really marvelous!

So, my dears, since this old lady seems to be still hitting on all six cylinders you will I hope excuse my occasional lapses of attention! They only seem like lapses, as I think of you oftener than I write—and send fond wishes,

"Mom" Murphy

Parenthood, even for the most devoted is only a part of life: independent, non-child–oriented existence has to be sustained afterward. Generally parents of one may realize this better than parents of more; certainly, this mother of one is living out such a realization well.

Chapter 6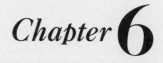

Is One Child for You?

If you presently have no children, we must of course begin with a more basic question: Is *any* child for you? Do you see any reason to become a parent?

In his essay "The Value of Children," Bernard Berelson lists four categories of reasons to have children:

Political reasons (to add to national strength)

Economic reasons (labor in the fields, dowry or "bride-wealth," care in later life)

Familial reasons (to continue family line or family name, religion or tradition)

Personal reasons (to provide a sense of personal competence, personal extension, personal experience, personal pleasure)

Political "reasons" for having children are clearly not so much real *reasons* as innocent citizen responses to outside forces. From Hammurabi to Hitler, expansionist leaders have defined reproduction as a duty. Fathers of many children were often exempt from taxation, mothers were given medals. Though such political reasons for having children may seem on the wane today (one almost never hears a prospective parent explain a coming childbirth as a patriotic act) there are lingering policy and attitude links between childbearing and "what's good for the country." Preferential treatment for parents remains, notably in the form of tax exemptions for progeny; and as recently as 1970 a U.S. President telephoned a mother to congratulate her on the birth of her eleventh child.

Why are political incentives for large families declining? Military strength for better or worse now depends less and less on numbers of men. Even expansionist leaders don't need mass armies, knowing well that any war of the future could conceivably be fought by two individuals, each facing a control panel with a red button. Thus the dissolution of this set of childbearing motives seems to be occurring *not* because they were recognized as unjust, from-above interference with what should be a purely personal decision—they simply have become outmoded.

"Economic" reasons are also shifting; indeed, at least in the developed world they have *already* shifted into ambiguity, and are moving quickly toward obsolescence. Married couples in India, in isolated areas untouched by government population policy messages, may still believe the old Indian saying, "Every new mouth to feed brings two hands to work," but in America almost everyone has figured out that children *cost*—they do not pay. Even in later life, old-age support now comes from social security systems, which, though flawed, are probably no less unreliable than children borne for the purpose of late-life "insurance."

"Familial" reasons persist. Though family rituals for which a child was needed (the Hindu son to light the father's funeral pyre, the Jewish son to recite Kaddish) are becoming rarer observances, a sense of obligation to "carry on the family line" lingers—but it too is fading. Anyone who dares state this as a reason for wanting to have a child risks being accused of "genetic narcissism," or some like term. One irreverent young son was heard to defy his family by saying, "All right, so what if I *do* have children to carry on the family line? Then what if *they* don't want to have children? Since *I* cannot guarantee *their* cooperation, can we please stop this 'Pass the Ego' game *now?*"

The most important category of contemporary motives is clearly the personal. Parenthood still generally confers status, guarantees attention, brings with it showers and flowers, ceremonies and celebrations. Parenthood does offer an opportunity for a creative experience. The challenge to shape a human life and guide a growing personality is deeply alluring even to many people who exercise creative roles in other ways. And for those who feel a definite liking for children, that fact alone can easily seem sufficient personal reason.

However, unlike the demographic dynamic underlying the "national strength" category of reasons for childbearing, which were unarguable (when strength relied on numbers, that was somehow *that*. Who could say that strength did not?), any personal reasons for wanting children can be challenged.

Further, they not only can be challenged—they should be, as strongly as possible; if, that is, we value the lives of children and indeed our own. The closer we can come to playing Perry Mason when confronted with a friend's personal testimony about wanting children, the greater the likelihood of preventing the disillusioned mutterings a few years later, "Damn. Who said this parenthood business was so damn glorious?" Not us.

The point of challenging anyone's stated reasons for child-wanting is not to distinguish between right and wrong reasons (if indeed such an easy distinction exists) but to sort out reasons which are *real* from those which are *illusory*, which have a quality of illogic or even self-deception about them. And the truth is that when most people explain why they feel they want a child, they are *not* explaining why they want a child at all. They are repeating something someone told them long ago.

There is, for instance, an entire set of explanations for reproduction usually expressed as admiration for certain qualities of children. Expressed in a simple statement, this argument runs, "Children are so _____" (innocent, natural, honest, spontaneous, unaffected, loving, etc.). I worry about men and women who expect to give birth to such a paragon. *Some* of the children are that way, *some* of the time. But it would be equally correct to say "Children are so _____" (selfish, noisy, demanding, irrational, or cruel to animals and each other).

The hope being expressed here is that the *adult* will personally again acquire some of the qualities of childhood most remembered or most desired: become less rigid, more spontaneous, perhaps. Again, *some* parents may reacquire such qualities, *some* of the time! "It is more likely," says a director of the Parental Stress Hot Line in Palo Alto, "that a parent will react to a child's spontaneity with increased tension. Adult life must contain a great deal of order and discipline. Is a parent going to react to the 'spontaneity' of a toddler rambling unpredictably toward breakable objects? Seldom!"

"Recaptured spontaneity" was the pronatalist argument seized on during a Pittsburgh talk show when a mother was trying to convince a confirmed male non-parent to have a child. "Yesterday," said the mother, "I took my five-year-old for a walk. As I saw her delight in every thing—the leaves, the trees, the flowers, the air, the sights and sounds of spring—I too felt such a boundless delight in the beauty of the day as I had not experienced since I myself was five." The non-parent seemed shocked.

"I honestly don't understand," he said. "I've never stopped being delighted at nature and the out of doors. And I attribute this to my not being responsible for a child every time I go for a hike. It's our own fault if any of us lose our childhood senses. And it's up to *us* if we want to get them back."

"Wanting to give" and "needing to prove" types of reasons easily devolve to feelings of insecurity, according to many psychologists. Dr. Herbert Robbins explains, "If a man says he wants to have a child because 'he can afford it,' he wants the child as a symbol of status, proof of his achieved income level. Or, if he says he wants to have a child because he 'wants to give his wife' a child, he may have the uneasy feeling that he personally is not giving her enough."

And as for having a child to keep a marriage together? That just might work for two unemployed pediatricians! Where the normal population is concerned, *it does not work.* Marriages without children are shown to be *happier* than those with children; in the period after childbirth, marital satisfaction not only generally *declines,* but this period represents a peak period of marital breakup.

Even "wanting to care for children," though that sounds as good or better than any other reason, when given as explanation for having one's own child, can have its darker side—of indicating a need for power over a dependent being or needing the presence of someone helpless in order to make oneself feel worthy or powerful. If one wants to care for children, there are ways to do so unrelated to the reproductive, after all.

Perhaps a desire underlying any personal reason for having children has something to do with wanting *permanence* in a swiftly changing world.

We have become a nation of transients, and face a future that looks ever more fluid. Somewhere, the generations of our mother's family and our father's family grew up, but we do not live there anymore. We live, perhaps, in Boston. But we have a summer place, and travel often on business. (How many of us who travel have ever awakened and not known where we were?) And if we live in Boston, it is not even a permanent Boston. Solid though they seem, the buildings around us move.

There is a story of a little girl in New York who was lost for two days while on an errand to the grocery store. Not only had the A&P fallen to the wrecking ball since her visit the week before, but enough shops had changed hands, enough structures and signs had mutated, that, lacking landmarks, she simply could not find her way home. Perhaps she even had no faith that home would still be there.

In one southern California county, the average marriage lasts eight months. The typical American will move ten times a lifetime. Given a world so transitory and untrustworthy, we all to some extent feel what a poet called "the universal human yearning for something permanent, enduring."

And perhaps, caught in unruly cultural currents, women (and men) seek some emotional anchor: something securing, self-defining. What better anchor than parenthood? For however the symbolic meaning of children may be individually interpreted, children universally offer *stasis.* What other role lasts forever? Not worker, seldom wife—and few liaisons of love or friendship survive the natural erosions of mobility and circumstance. But having given birth, one will never again *not be* a parent.

Still, the hope of achieving something permanent by taking on the role of parent is somewhat illusory. Usually such hopes are based on more or less specific (if unconscious) expectations that the child will carry on work we have begun or values that are ours. Or an ancillary kind of permanence is hoped for: marital, say . . .

This reason, too, is vulnerable.

What then?

"We owe our parents a grandchild." *(Why?)*

"We adore children." *(Of what ages?)*

Is there *any* reason to have a child?

Admittedly paraphrasing a classic detective-story distinction, one psychologist answered that question by saying, "There is never a reason for parenthood—there is only a motive."

Dr. Benjamin Spock has gone right to the heart of this quandary by declaring, "Only those people who can't resist having children should have them. There's no practical reason ever to have children."

Other psychologists and authorities agree that motivations for parenthood have no rational basis, only an emotional one.

But if you have one child, you've resolved all this rhetoric into a commitment to parenthood, and the question "Is one child for you?" becomes, more accurately, "Is a *second* child for you?" For you, since you have one child, diffuse and subtle reasons for reproduction which touch on generativity and identity are satisfied. Motives for further children should be a little easier to examine and identify.

If you already have one child, is one child for you?

The following checklist, expanded with discussion, has been compiled from a number of authorities:

IS ONE CHILD FOR YOU?

1. YES, *if* you are considering a second child in order to conform to what is socially proper or socially expected. Conformity is a poor reason for a second child. Social expectations? Will the society who expects the second child raise it? Or will you? Yet Dr. Charles Arnold of the American Health Foundation is not alone in pointing out that "Expectations are powerful, and most people are made to *expect* to have two children." If you are only responding to an impulse to conform to some ideal picture of "what a family *should* be like," be careful. Arnold and others point out that women may feel committed to have the same number of children their mother had (even Alice Ginott has stated that initially, "I wanted four children, because my mother had four children. Do you see how irrational it all is?"), and men may be vulnerable to particular kinds of career-image motives. Just as a man may find that being a husband supports his professional role, he may imagine that being the father of the "traditional" two-child family

will burnish that image to a high gloss. "There are a lot of 'corporate children,' " says one industrial psychologist.

IS ONE CHILD FOR YOU?

2. YES, *if* your motive for more than one is to "escape" from the intimacy the one-child family offers as one of its best, most meaningful features. This is a "hidden" motive, not easy to detect. (But it is certainly obvious, given the flurry of new intimacy-achieving workshops, that many adults do have conflict about entering into close relationships.) Do you feel stifled, "too close" to your family members, your spouse and child? Just as parents can have *one* child to distract them from the need for unrelieved intimacy with each other in their household, so they can unconsciously want a second child *to lessen their degree of commitment to and involvement with the first.* Is this a good reason to have a second child? Are there alternatives for achieving the balance of closeness/distance you want to have with your family members?

IS ONE CHILD FOR YOU?

3. YES, *if* you are considering a second child *only* in order to *avoid an only!* Researchers who prepared a special study on "Social and Psychological Factors Affecting Fertility"[1] concluded that "It is clear that 'not wanting an only child figures prominently as a major encouragement for having the second child." The strength of this motive is indicated by the following percentages of husbands and wives holding it!

	Wives	*Husbands*
High socioeconomic status	89%	90%
Medium socioeconomic status	68%	52%
Low socioeconomic status	67%	66%

(For reasons unknown, the higher-status couples were most frequently influenced by this motive.)

Are you among this group? Do you believe an only child is handicapped in any way (despite certain undeniable advantages)? Are there ways to deal with any problems you think characteristic of the only child *without* providing a sibling? Almost all of the most respected authorities in the field of family science today feel that any child deserves to be wanted for himself—*not* to satisfy what are presumed to be the needs of an older child.

IS ONE CHILD FOR YOU?

4. YES, *if* you are considering a second child because your only child has asked for a sibling! It is the rare parent of an only child who does not feel a flash of guilt when this occurs. (Notice we said *when* this occurs, not *if* this occurs, because it almost invariably does—especially when it rains.) However, it is highly unlikely that your only child really wants a sibling. He or she may well be curious, and wonder what it would be like, but *that* is about as deep as the feeling goes. It's well to know that this "desire" can be expected at predictable times—whenever, for instance, a friend of your only child gets a new brother or sister. And it's also good to be alert to the fact that your only child may have

been "set up" for the request by outside forces: "Why don't you tell your mother and father you'd like a little brother or sister?"

If the expressed desire does seem to be spontaneous, not urged by others, then what your only child is asking for is a playmate. Find one.

This can also be a good opportunity to educate an only child as to what sibling relationships are really like, and what an infant really is. Point out how friends of his with younger or older siblings relate (or don't) and acquaint him with a neighborhood newborn in as intimate a way as possible—including the feedings, the crying, and the things he may not have thought of as occurring. Explain that "If you had a brother or sister this is what he or she would be like for a long time." You might also (suggests the wise mother of an only child who did just this) explain to your only child why he is enough for you.

IS ONE CHILD FOR YOU?

5. YES, *if* you are considering a second child because you want another *baby*. Parenthood is obviously not the same game through all its innings. The psychological adjustment, for instance, is usually greatest in the very first months of an infant's life ("I'm frightened every time I look at the baby and think, 'This responsibility is mine *forever*,' " said a new father, not atypically), but the financial impact is not at its height until the teenage years. Many kinds of adjustments thus have to be weighed. Having adjusted to an infant, it might seem easy to "add another." But have you considered the

cost. It's difficult to foresee the financial burden you will get with a second child (because you haven't experienced the full impact of that yet) but relatively easy to feel that you have "mastered" the infant stage; and, like an "expert," want to try it again.

Then, too, many women have been conditioned and socialized to respond to infants only (or to infants primarily). Losing a cuddly baby and gaining a querulous toddler may seem surprising, provoke a feeling that the mother has "lost" her baby. The consensus of advice seems to be this: If it is the cuddling and infant care you miss, you're courting neglect *of your older child* by having a new baby. You will be very tempted to shortchange the older one in the thrill of again doing what you feel you do best: responding to what was so recently so familiar and satisfying—the relatively simple, if tiring, tasks of feeding, cuddling, changing.

IS ONE CHILD FOR YOU?

6. YES, *if* you want to have a second child "in case the first one dies." The first few years of a child's life are most prone to tragic accidents or sudden death, the health authorities point out. If you have gotten your child to age three or four, you can feel relatively secure about his survival into adulthood. There is never any guarantee, of course, but neither is there any guarantee, if you had a second child, that *both* children would not be together on the same ill-fated bus or airplane. And a child is a unique human being; surely no younger child you had could "replace" or "substitute for" the one you have now? When their beloved only

son Leland died in 1884, Jane Lathrop Stanford and her husband said, "The children of California shall be our children," and seven years later Stanford University became a reality, founded with the money that would have been their son's inheritance—and founded also, as the university's first president so often stressed, with love.

IS ONE CHILD FOR YOU?

7. YES, *if* you are considering a second child because you believe *the second is easier* and thus you "might as well" have another.

"The second *is* easier," said a demographer, his tone of voice disclosing that he knew what he was about to say by heart and trusted all to be impressed. "After all, the difference between zero and one is infinity. The difference between one and two is only a hundred percent. Thus, in terms of time," he continued, "if Child A takes x hours of work, assigning to x an arbitrary value of, say, six, then some of those x (six) hours could automatically serve any other child, say Child B, that was around. I am thinking specifically of meal preparation, here. But the application of the same principle in other areas could easily mean that the value of the y hours when they were finally calculated to indicate time exclusively devoted to Child B would clearly put the y figure below x."

I could almost see a magazine article forming in his mind as he spoke. I only hope he writes it for *Modern Math Today,* not for any journal that purports to speak responsibly to mothers.

If a child were a mathematical constant, the demographer might be correct. But no such thing can be assumed at all.

The second is easier? Maybe the second Channel crossing is easier. Maybe the second chocolate soufflé is easier. But the *second child?* "Almost nobody believes that," says Rebecca Liswood. "That's an 'official press release' reason people give, not the real one. It's an explanation so familiar that anyone stating it feels comfortable, knowing no one is likely to question it. Sometimes this is a parent's coverup for wanting to get locked into the parent role rather than investigate alternatives—an 'escape from freedom' dynamic. And sometimes it's just an indication that the real reason hasn't been thought about at all."

"The second is *not* easier," Jessie Bernard firmly believes. "It is not even just twice as much work—the work increases, often, by about a factor of four. Being responsible for two is more than twice the job of being responsible for one. The physical workload may *merely* double, but the emotional factor more than does so. If you were just overseeing the growth dynamics, the personality emergence, the social adjustment, the problems of two individual children it might be twice as much work. But in addition you have to oversee their relationship to each other, their relationships to others not just individually but as a team, how their individual constellations of friendships merge or conflict. It becomes enormously more demanding."

Alice Rossi too has found that "For mothers, adjustment problems are greater with multipara [second or later births] than with primapara [first births]." And

Dr. Rossi reports observing this in all occupational and social spheres, among women of all ages, among both private and clinic patients.

Recent research by ZPG found that mothers of one child talked positively about motherhood, but mothers of two or more mentioned expense, fatigue, the weight of responsibility, and other negative factors.

Finally, a California author and mother of two, Shirley Radl, had this to say: "The idea that the second child is easier is one of those simplistic one-liners that has a nice ring to it, but falls to pieces when put to the test of actual experience. Sometimes, the second *birth* is easier. And sometimes, *physical care* of a second baby is easier now that Mom has been through basic training. But at least giving physical care to the *first* infant could be done without distractions—that's not the case now. And what if the second baby isn't as happy or healthy or easy to care for as the first? A fussy or sickly baby would drive 'the second is easier' idea to the used-theories lot."

Radl and mothers she has interviewed emphasize too that unless your two children are very alike in personality and energy you can be pulled apart by their differing needs.

Even physical safety can seem jeopardized. What's a mother to do when she is bathing the baby and suddenly realizes her four-year-old is on the roof? What is she to do when changing the baby if her older one has just figured out how to open the childproofed front door and is heading out into traffic?

But the most profound difficulties are doubtless those pointed to by Bernard—the tasks of socializing two children. Moving from one to two children can easily move the socializing responsibility from the realm of the possible to that of the overwhelming.

IS ONE CHILD FOR YOU?

8. YES, *if* you are considering a second child because you believe *"they'll be playmates."* Why does a child need a built-in playmate? Why do you feel *your* child wants or needs or should have one? Are you by any chance thinking, unconsciously, "As I parent I don't offer my only child enough. Another child will make up for the time I don't want to give"?

"But my child says frequently, 'I don't have anyone to play with,'" a mother of an only will occasionally say. *She,* however, probably hears this less often than mothers of more than one. Mothers of two, three, or more report the no-playmate complaint most frequently, according to Shirley Radl, who adds, "A suggestion that the playmateless child do something with a nearby brother or sister is met with the reaction that mother has gone out of her mind."

Siblings *do* play together sometimes—more often during the ages six to twelve than earlier or later—and if recreational facilities, *outdoors,* are set up to encourage this.

But siblings are very seldom the kind of playmates who can also be called friends. The reason for this is simple: Children learn most about themselves from someone else their *own* age. That's why at any playground or situation where children come together in a group, five-year-olds immediately seek out other five-year-olds, seven-year-olds play with other seven-year-olds, etc.

Siblings cannot be playmates and friends because they are anxious rivals, most authorities agree. "Come to my office and see sibling rivalry among children," invites Rebecca Liswood. "Then listen to the children after they leave my office; hear how often they refer to their sibling as 'My bratty brother,' 'My snotty kid sister.' " And when the siblings are very close in age and therefore might most easily share play *interests,* the rivalry is most intense. On the other hand, if the age levels differ, the play needs will be incompatible. (Margaret Mead, having been promised a playmate, found her new baby brother "exasperatingly" inept at that task. "Can't he say anything but da-da-da all the time?" she remembers asking.)

And young Alvin Toffler's disappointment at seeing a new baby brought home was clear—"I wanted a puppy," he said.

Often, in fact, play between siblings calls forth an unexpected hobby-horse from the playroom corner. Rivalry rears its ugly head. Playing with blocks *can* mean the cooperative planning and building of a miniature castle or town hall, sure; it can also mean using the blocks as weapons for direct hitting or throwing. One positive effect may be practice in hand-eye coordination. But the much greater negative effect is that such quarrels are not forgotten by young children but build into a pattern of petty violence that perpetuates itself. ("The next time I hit him I won't miss" paves the way for a "next time.")

Another form of play that is common (chasing one

another through the house or apartment) can also involve a power struggle. And it holds astonishing potential for destruction.

The firm instruction to "play quietly in your room," says a mother who considers her household typical in its sibling conflicts, "puts two children in a space that, no matter how large or small, is eventually not big enough for both of them. They then find various ways of letting each other know this. They are heard arguing over which program to watch, hitting and kicking each other to make their respective points, hurling insults, screaming, and running to mother to settle whatever the grievance may be."

As siblings grow older, differences in temperament, energy, and personality may turn into genuine value conflicts. These are often not talked over, but acted out. In a household with two adolescents, one traditional, the other more of an experimenter with whatever's-going-on, one "tells," the other "retaliates." It's true enough that sometimes siblings who fought violently for fifteen years become friends as adults. But there are just as many relationships that are characterized by a literal stand-off. Enmity is not unknown. As one elder brother put it, "Just because you're born related to somebody doesn't mean you're going to like them."

IS ONE CHILD FOR YOU?

9. YES, *if* you feel in any way "disappointed" with your first child, or with parenthood. Lois Wyatt and Frederick Hoffman of the University of Michigan have

pointed out that a common cause of a second child is a parental response of disillusionment or inadequacy to their *present* situation. Some parents feel they have not done a "good enough job" with their first (and can make up for this by a superior performance the second time around). Others feel their child is in some way a disappointment, not all they had hoped for (and their second will be brighter, more outgoing, more cooperative, whatever). These are compensatory motives, and risky ones. They skirt the parents' central need for self-analysis just as surely as "running away" from the situation would. "Getting in deeper" is merely their way of "running away" rather than facing things as they are with a conscious effort to change the existing family constellation, by attitude, action, or perhaps simply *patience.* All families go through rough periods, all children go through difficult phases. The desire to have a second child may be no more than a reaction to temporary difficulties.

IS ONE CHILD FOR YOU?

10. YES, *if* you feel a second child "would make no difference to the way we live now." This is an illusion. Much that is explored in the field of family size and family dynamics, filled with complicated questions as it is, must be qualified ("if," "maybe," "sometimes"). But it can be firmly predicted that *a second child will change things.* It will, in fact, change everything—from getting breakfast to future career plans and area of residence. (A second child will even greatly change your first child.) *If* a couple has been fortunate (as many couples

who have one child are, because a lot of fortune comes with the situation) in adjusting to one child easily, it's tempting to think that another child, too, would add himself to the family structure with no disruption. Try to think of ways in which the second child would change your lives—then ask if you are prepared to face those changes.

IS ONE CHILD FOR YOU?

11. YES, *if* you want a second child for "something more to do." In the past, when birth control had begun to emancipate women reproductively but women's liberation had not yet offered activity *economically,* excess fertility was often a function of leisure time. Explore alternate ways to fill time—productively, not reproductively.

IS ONE CHILD FOR YOU?

YES, until you and your spouse or partner have together considered the following:
1. Have we considered our "real" reason for wanting a second child?
2. Have we calculated the cost of having a second child?
3. Have we discussed the impact a second child would have on our present life-style? (Think of your family and individual activities during an ordinary week. How might these have to be modified?)
4. Do both of you remember clearly what caring for a new baby is like?
5. Do you feel you have enough "extra" time and energy to deal with a second child?

6. Are you satisfied with your present pattern of sharing responsibility for taking care of the child you have? Have you discussed how responsibility for the second would be shared?

7. Would the place where you now live accommodate a second child? Until what age? Are you prepared to move? Where?

8. Do you feel that you now have enough privacy? too little? more than enough? How would a second child affect the quality of your time together?

9. Have you spoken personally, with those whose candor you trust, with parents of one child and parents of two children?

10. What are your *standards* for "providing well" for your child or children? (With one child, you can assure perhaps not only college but any postgraduate or special professional training. With two, you might be able to assure undergraduate education only.)

11. Have you considered adopting a child?

12. Do you feel you could learn to "distribute" love and attention equitably?

13. Have you considered the nature of the child you now have and how he or she might be affected by a sibling?

14. Have you discussed the possibility of a sibling with the child you now have? Are you sure your present child understands relatively well what a new baby would mean? (Be sure you do not promise a "playmate" or your child will be disappointed!) Be sure that your child understands that any new brother or sister will be coming to your house for more than "a visit."

15. Are you simply "trying for a boy/girl"? *Why?*

IS ONE CHILD FOR YOU?

YES, if you can identify with any of the following usual reasons parents of one have given for deciding to have an only child:

"After the birth of my daughter, who was unusually bright (she could add numbers at twelve months and recite nursery rhymes at fourteen months) I realized that I had 'hit the jackpot' and wanted to devote my full energies to nurturing this gifted child. However, even had she not been gifted, I would not have had the emotional strength to do a good job of raising more than one."

"I hate being busy and rushed. Don't know if this is limited patience or low energy but I love it when life seems relaxed. With more children I doubt I'd be a good mother but a mean and cross one. I have enough trouble coping with *one* well-behaved, extraordinarily controlled kid! A second would clearly spell disaster."

"We are lovers of peace and quiet and believe that having an only child has freed us from years of sibling fights."

"We automatically started to discuss a second child after our first was born. Soon we discovered the only reason we would have another child would be to give Heather a brother or sister. We decided that was a terrible reason to have a child—so we didn't do it."

"Though our baby was good, it became more and more apparent that neither of us particularly enjoyed all the work involved with children or the lack of time by ourselves. The recognition that children just weren't our thing produced an increasingly firm desire to *not* have another. By the time he was two we knew he would be an only child. And our own attitude toward parenthood improved somewhat, since we knew there would be no additional demands. We began to appreciate our son more."

"The selfishness of having more children when there are millions of children starving and homeless is appalling. We *might* adopt another but want to give our daughter many good years as our 'only' first. Then if we adopt, the three of us will make that decision jointly."

"We originally planned to have two children six years apart. Our reflections on our own childhoods plus my observations as a teacher led us to believe that the intense rivalry between sibs was not desirable. At the same time we realized we had probably only 'wanted' two because it was socially acceptable. We decided to stay with what was *personally* acceptable."

"Our home is quiet and orderly. We like that."

"I wanted to return to a profession. I was able to do so more easily with one child."

"With one, we seem to retain both our serenity and sense of humor (which we have often seen parents lose). I think we nag and frown less than parents with more children."

"Financially, we are ahead. We are building a home, no mortgage, have just finished our college educations at night school. Can take vacations and travel with less hassle, are more free to live our own lives. We feel *pretty confident* that we can provide for Ben the kind of life we want for him. With another, we would feel less sure of our ability to do so."

"We have been able to offer our child every advantage. She has had exposure to many learning experiences: classes at nature center, art and language lessons, swimming and tennis. She has had the quiet time to read and create at her leisure. She will continue to have advantages of education, time, love, attention and effort on our part. Whatever she becomes, we will at least know in our hearts that we gave her every chance."

"Nothing seems worse to my wife and me than dependency in our old age—on charity, government, social security, or even our own family. We have a savings plan and stocks that will assure taking care of ourselves."

"I was given a new little person who is a wonderful puzzle box, full of surprises. I don't want to miss even the smallest facet of her delightful emergence by being preoccupied with other puzzle boxes."

"No matter how much a man and woman love each other, the times we live in make separation or divorce a real possibility. If I were ever a single parent, I could care for one child. I could not care for more. People have told me this kind of thinking is negative and pessimistic. I think it's practical."

"My husband and I have little privacy in spite of geographical separation from our own brothers and sisters. They have time to write *us* long letters and feel offended if we do not reply in kind or even if we phone instead. So many gifts are obligatory to young nieces and nephews. We have discussed this with our only daughter, Lynn. Will you be sad not to have so many relatives when you grow up? we have asked her. She sees her onliness as an advantage. So do we."

"Frankly—to be very blunt—we saw our neighbors start screaming after the second one."

"It's a special experience—I only wanted it once."

Finally, one parent wrote, "It comes down to this. *Who* would benefit if we had a second child? We decided that we would not. All right then, would our *child* gain anything that we could not provide otherwise? He would gain, if things turned out ideally, a loving companion and friend. Certainly, there are other sources for those: blood kin have no corner on brotherly love. Would society gain? At best, society would gain a good citizen. But without another child *we* have time to be better citizens and be more alert to issues which concern all of us. We can also help our one child to become a better citizen and help maximize his education and desire to do so. For whose good then? The unconceived child's? The very idea is either metaphysical, or absurd.

"We will stay as we are."

Is one child for you? I don't really know the answer to that question any more than your next-door neighbor does. I only hope that I may have served a purpose in counteracting what your next-door neighbor (and just about everyone else) has been telling you so that, having heard all positions on some of the key issues involved, you can turn to yourself for the final answer.

I think one child *is* for you *if* you have been significantly affected by the preceding questions. The questions offer no guarantee that your decision will be either right or rational —but they should improve the chances. But just as there is probably no practical or rational reason for having a first child (but only a set of emotional dynamics), so too, if you decide to have a second child, you may also be following an emotional prompter, not a rational one.

But there's this at least: Having read all the arguments against the idea, if you still want a second child, at least the strength of your emotional desire has been measured. And that desire may do a great deal to see you through.

Chapter 7

The Family of the Future: The One-child Family

Birth and *the future* are close kin: siblings, rivals. We are just beginning to sense the full dangers of their conflict, realizing with no little apprehension that the outcome of their struggle to achieve opposed objectives will determine the nature of continued life on earth. One requires stasis. The dynamics of the other are bent inexorably on growth. (And growth continues, despite the heralded declines in birth rates lately. An elementary principle of math is that *rates* have *bases;* and our base population is now so large that, even at the lowered rate, we added numbers equal to Los Angeles and environs last year.) Worldwide, the problem is compounded. The future is no longer unassailable. Too high a continuing reproductive challenge will render it infirm, even lifeless—the stuff of bad dreams.

What got us here? The extravagant fertility of past generations? Sure. That answer is easy and correct, but also a little off the mark, unfair. We could, were we so inclined, "blame" our present ecological problems on a lack of "responsibility" for the future on the part of past generations. And it's true enough that had a small family norm existed one hundred years ago—when our U.S. population was a mere benign 19 million, not today's 200 million—it would have left to us a heritage not so marked by pollution, crowding, and other ominous global problems.

My great-grandmother did not know this. Measuring "the future" in days or seasons, those of her generation had their children (eight was usual) as most of the women of all earth's cultures have had them: inevitably, reflexively, unthinkingly—the biological consequence of married rural life. Though historians have sometimes remarked that large families have been a gesture of faith in the future, I think this too poetic. Based as it may have been on an assumption too obvious to need articulation (that there would *be* a future), this exercise of fertility was still likely no "gesture of faith." It was simply done.

My great-grandmother lived after Malthus wrote and when a German zoologist named Ernst Haeckel coined the word "ecology," but I believe she never heard of them. And what if she had?

What if some student of Malthus had traveled by horseback to the homesteads of all the pioneering families in the 1870s to warn young wives that their family size could cause the genesis of fearsome land-use questions and labor-resource imbalances years hence? What if he had sternly explained that without care the number of their children would stimulate a *twelvefold* increase in U.S. numbers (and be part of the critical second billion-doubling worldwide)? My great-grandmother would have been polite. But she, I think, would still have had eight children.

Large families offered, then, companionability in isolated settlements, more agrarian productivity and thus prosperity, and old-age security at a time when it was not offered by bureaucracies—only by sons.

Even had the threats of high fertility been known, the threats they posed to the "future" stood opposed to the benefits accrued in the then "present." The world view of population dangers was at odds with private comfort and well-being.

The large family was a function of an agricultural time. Future aside, a small family would have seemed antithetical to that time. The needs and dimensions of the way-it-was-then were sufficient to obscure even a *concept* of a future very far removed, for we were only 19 million then and there were over five hundred acres of land for every one of us. What was "the future" anyway, except to fill that land?

But we are not in an agricultural era now, and things will never be again the way they were a century ago, or even yesterday. With communications and technology, the future has grown ever closer. We live in it, and Malthusian messengers visit us electronically very often, warning us of dangers of high fertility. Since high fertility is always subject to functional redefinition, a high-fertility family in the United States is coming to mean *a couple with two children!*

What non-parenthood and one-child families represent might almost be seen as a "reverse pioneer" movement that is no less significant than Manifest Destiny. Increasingly, we will limit our fertility to such low levels *now* because the needs of the future are, *now,* consonant with our own advantages. Even those who still do not "see" the future (or who have a "What has posterity ever done for me?" attitude) recognize that the smallest of families means no less companionability, security, identity. So our fertility patterns are contracting, not expanding. And we are not seeking out unpeopled rural territory, for it is not there: It is now Omaha. We are converging into Omaha, and cities of all sizes (into cities of a half million to 600,000 most quickly). We are urbanizing.

We are urbanizing because we have little choice (high-density housing is land-conserving, and anyway our economic unit is no longer the family but the corporation), and an urban area favors child-free or one-child families. A city is just not conducive to multiple children, for children in multiples are already there, and there is restricted space.

This is one reason why Marguerite Krebs believes, "It is clear that the only child is the child of the future. Once, when society was small and families lived far apart, the large family offered the advantage of socialization. Single-child families would not have made sense. Today, they do."

Jessie Bernard feels the space factor to be critical. "The population of this country has tripled in my lifetime," she reflects, "and a major consequence has been space restriction. At one time, those who immigrated to this country may have been used to crowded conditions in cities and were not hindered from having large families by lack of space, privacy . . . but somewhere along the way Americans got used to space and privacy. Knowing that all family members might have to live and grow up in space equivalent to one small apartment will definitely influence future family size."

Crowding begets a kind of commonality. We are seeing this already. Urban environments are communal in that we share buildings, transportation, recreational facilities—*and* children. Sharing of children among couples, among women, through cooperative day care provides an abundance of what might be called *semisiblings*. This plays a major role in making an only child seem "enough."

If the only child might appear to call for supplementary socialization from sources other than his small, nuclear family unit, there seems small worry this will be provided. "If the one-child trend develops," foresees René Dubos, "a mechanism will occur which will richly socialize that child. Human beings are much more inventive of social mechanisms than is generally believed. It may take as long as one generation to get a new social mechanism operating, sometimes not that long. Something interesting is happening in apartment buildings already. A mother with one child sees another mother with one child. How rapidly they enter into a relationship! A few more additions, and the result is almost like an extended family of the past." Other informal movements to extend families result from feminist groups, churches. The intent is to form associations in which couples (young or old; with one child, none, or more), single parents, grandparents, people from any style of life, join together for holidays and keep in touch with one another generally. "That behavior is familial," says Bernard.

For the only child, these networks offer wide friendships, companionships. The only child has access to such socialization opportunities, and he will have an important advantage over children from larger families in that *he can get away from the socialization*. To him will be available *some* private space, *some* quiet place, and the security of a small unit as a retreat from the dark side of socialization, which is properly called overcrowding.

With his quiet home as an escape from the stresses, noise, and overstimulation of the outside urban world, he will have a better chance to avoid that withdrawal syndrome that urban planner Christopher Alexander has called "one of the worst consequences of modern life." But if withdrawal is "one of the worst" consequences, it's not the only bad one. Following experimental studies to explore the relationship between anonymity and aggression, Stanford psychologist P.G. Zimbardo stopped just short of concluding that urban pressures are transforming Americans into potential assassins.[1]

The deleterious effects of too-great numbers to planetary parameters have been well-documented, with resource depletion, crowding, and famine the most obvious manifestations. But living among too many others does *personal* harm as well, and can "crowd" or "starve" or distort areas of personality and potential creativity. James S. Plant, a psychiatrist who has worked extensively in juvenile clinics in the New York–New Jersey area, is only representative of a near-consensus among professionals who believe overcrowding to have negative effects on mental health. With little or no personal privacy, there is little or no chance to develop a sense of individuality or to look objectively at oneself. Instead, writes Plant, there is a preoccupying tension and strain of constantly having to get along with others.[2] "Pernicious" is a word Albert Ellis uses to describe potential effects of crowding in one's personal environment; in particular, "Young children take it badly."

"Children today face overcrowding, oversocialization," observes Krebs, "and tomorrow's society will be even more complex. The most valuable gift parents can give a child today is privacy. Parents of an only child are much, much better able to insure their child that advantage."

Julie A. Cleare (who believes, pioneer expansionist thinking aside, we have always in the past produced far more children than anyone really wanted) joins Krebs in foreseeing the one-child family as a new norm. "Both because of privacy, and greater opportunity for parental intimacy to be seen undisturbed by greater numbers of children, the only child in the future could have an edge in learning how to develop *intimacy* in a world which will be increasingly short on long, intimate relationships and abundant in short, choppy ones: too many contacts for too short a duration."

Technology plays a role in this, a role in devaluing what is intimate or natural, human or small scale, we are sometimes told. And in an anomalous way it does. Industrial technology has fragmented job functions, fractured the "whole" worker or craftsman, replaced the generalist with the narrow specialist. But medical technology (birth control) has made possible the smaller, closer, *less* fragmented family. (Large families scatter, electrons in unrelated orbits, maybe leaving notes for one another. It's hard for a family of two or three to fragment: Each depends on another.)

And medical technology has set things up well for the emergence of those two- or three-person families. Birth control. The assurance of the survival of an only child. Though not widely known, the technology exists today to predetermine the sex of a child—surely a profoundly important benefit to those who want just one.

The way the economy in contemporary life works (or doesn't) also seems set up to make the one-child family seem eminently desirable, *practical.* "It's a big enough job right now just supporting ourselves, let alone children," is commonly heard from young couples.

There will doubtless be fewer and fewer economic certainties—partly because there will be fewer and fewer *environmental* ones. Economic activity is based on the exploitation of natural resources, converted in some way to products, with the resulting depletion of those resources *and* pollution caused by the energy transfer in the manufacture of those products. As Ralph Nader once put it very simply, "When the GNP goes up, the environment goes down." But there are unanswered questions as to what will happen as resources become scarce or exhausted . . . when pollution reaches unacceptable or intolerable levels. Lack of faith in governments and their monies, unprecedented international trading blocs also complicate the picture, making the future more than a little unpredictable. But a scenario such as Alvin Toffler creates in *The Eco-Spasm* report is not at all out of the realm of the possible:

> Suddenly a wave of personal bankruptcies sweeps through the nation, soaring to the rate of 60,000 per month, as dentists and dockworkers, young married couples and retirees find it impossible to pay their bills. A senator from California proposes creation of a Federal Loan Insurance Corporation to guarantee credit card companies and other lenders against bad debts so they can continue to extend credit to "keep the wheels of America moving." . . . Demand for bicycles is outrunning the industry's capacity to produce. 4,000 unemployed workers have turned up for 700 jobs. Scuffling turns into an ugly riot between whites and blacks and spills into the streets. By nightfall, a 6-block area of Cleveland is in flames and the National Guard cannot contain the rioting. . . . In Manhattan, the Excelsior Cooperative on 57th Street announces that its board of directors has authorized the purchase of a farm in upstate New York to provide "guaranteed food supplies, including dairy products," for the residents of the high-rise luxury building. Each

tenant is assessed $2000 for that purpose. In the future, when a tenant sells an apartment, shares will include part ownership of the farm.[3]

On the other hand, the one-child family offers both personal and systemic economic advantages. At the family level, there is only *one* dependent member to raise and educate—and (usually) *two* family members who are income-producing. This holds out almost optimum prosperity, exceeded only by child-free living units.

Nationally, the same picture would emerge, enlarged. We would experience a reduced need for population-related investments such as classrooms, buildings, and highways, and thereby make additional savings available for investments to increase the quality of life for the smaller population. We would *also* see an easing of the pressure to constantly expand the number of jobs in the country. The unemployment problem would virtually cease to nag us.

It is no coincidence that the highest employment rates are found in countries that are close to ZPG, such as Sweden, Germany, or Switzerland. In those countries, as a person retires, he is replaced by a younger worker just entering the labor force. Thus the employment picture is stable. (But when there are *more* people flowing into the labor force than retiring, the result is either unemployment or the necessity to create new jobs, and this begets either inflation, or tax burdens, or both.) Clearly, the stable-flow situation is preferable. In fact, the unemployment which has plagued the United States cyclically over past generations is identified by Professor Ed Passerini of the University of Alabama as resulting from the skewed capital-labor ratios which have been with us since the U.S. population passed 150 million!

There would be undeniable ecological advantages to population stabilization as well, and a one-child family average would make some of these environmental ameliorations *available in our lifetime.* With a two-child family average, demographers explain, growth and its attendant problems would continue well past the year 2000. In fact, given no significant immigration controls, with a two-child family average, the U.S. population might *never* stabilize!

However, if only an additional 15 percent of today's emerging families chose to have one child, we could well enjoy a stabilized population before the year 2000; and if as many as 40 percent of beginning families had one child only, our numbers might well stabilize within ten years.

The possibility is alluring to anyone who has had more than enough of *more*—more cities, more cars, more roads, more people, more products, more pollution, more everything. Presently, we all live under growth-related threats to our personal well-being. Every few weeks, there seems a dramatic new chemico-technological surprise: kepone in the Chesapeake Bay, dioxin-poisoned swaths of land marked by dead animals across Italy. Not only do massive, overwhelming numbers create a need for processes of chemistry and technology, numbers also make it difficult to untangle webs of vested interest and determine the true dimensions of such disasters. (The governors of Maryland and Virginia both claim kepone is affecting only the waters of the *other* state; citizens of Seveso watched death around them for seven days before evacuation of the area began. Douglas Davis of *Newsweek* lays the blame for the harm of "vast bureaucracies, a tidal wave of administrators" directly at the door of overpopulation.)

In interims between Sevesos, quieter processes of deterioration surround us. Suburbs leapfrog from center cities out to beltways and beyond, turning clusters of trees into exurban sprawl—and *every six months* we pave over an area of land roughly equal to the size of Rhode Island. This destruction of greenery means that, quietly, our air is growing thinner. LaMont Cole of Cornell University has calculated that for the forty-eight contiguous United States in 1966 oxygen production was only about 60 percent of the amount consumed.[4]

A single-child family norm would offer some respite from all this.

More women in the work force and changing women's roles generally also favor a single child per woman. As Cynthia Epstein and others have emphasized, the American conjugal family system has heavily weighted the woman's family role with child-rearing duties. The average mother (outside job or not) has a myriad of child-care tasks to perform during hours at home. Egalitarian sharing of work involved in house and child care may certainly emerge in the future; right now it seems at best a good-will effort attempted by some of the husbands, some of the time (and with much backsliding, feminists report). This may be why Susan Neisuler, Boston feminist and population activist, firmly characterizes the decision to limit the number of offspring per family to its absolute minimum—one—as "a personal, private, *female* decision. In countries where women are educated to the same degree as men are," she continues, "the longing to make use of that education is irresistible. One child means a much quicker, more manageable return to the professional working world." The trend will be circular, she predicts: As more and more children grow up and live satisfying lives as onlies, the women among these only children will turn increasingly to one-child families on reaching maturity.

Then, too, the blurring of sex roles will make it less important to have a "little man," a "male heir," a "John Jones III," a "son to carry on the family name." The *New York Times* recently carried a lengthy feature on small business across the nation in which a daughter—not a son—has joined Dad in the family enterprise. Indeed, "my daughter the doctor" may become an oft-heard revision of the traditional sexist cliché, as women increasingly desire—or indeed demand—their own adult fulfillment.

A place in the professional world isn't the only factor in adult fulfillment, certainly. And a change in our cultural values—a shift toward "self development," "personal growth," and continuing education *for adults*—seems to have a lot to do with an overall psychology that the demands of a large family would make impractical if not impossible. "Men and women today are more interested in direct experience and fulfillment," says Herbert Robbins, "and that is an important change from the thinking of adults in past generations who were content to settle for the vicarious satisfactions of watching their children achieve what they themselves had not."

The one-child family, agrees Alvin Toffler, represents a significant emancipation from the "fantastic immersion in the world of children" that characterized social acceptability until recently. "The child is still important to the adults, but the child's importance is more than occasionally subordinate to the goals of the adults."

Sacrificing "all" for your children seems definitely out of date, though this does not mean the child will suffer. Indeed, the child may be healthier for the de-emphasis on his needs exclusively, most psychologists believe. (One psychologist bluntly termed the old sacrifice-all-for-the-sake-of-the-children syndrome "pure masochism.")

The trend toward continuing enrichment or educational experiences for Mom or Dad can even teach a child, by example, that such experiences are meaningful and to be appreciated when they fall *his* way. (Almost thirty years ago, I remember a neighborhood friend demanding of her mother, "Why should I take piano lessons? *You* don't.") One reason the mother didn't, of course, was that she had resigned from active duty in the all-out effort to give her children "The Advantages," as they used to be called. Today, everyone in the family may be in on the pursuit of advantages. Piano lessons for Susie? French lessons for Mother? est for Dad? In a single-child family these questions are not strung together by "either/or." There are enough family resources—time, energy, money, motivation —to offer such advantages to all.

Family egalitarianism could emerge in a new dimension. The family is small enough not to be consumed in the "nuclear network" of multirelationships; its individuals are free to function independently in the pursuit of sustaining interests. This is not only the egalitarianism *between spouses* urged by feminists tired of male dominance. It is also egalitarianism *between generations,* representing a parallel emancipation from what might be called "child supremacy." Low fertility thus spells liberation for both spouses, bringing more control over their own lives and futures. In a world that seems increasingly *out* of control ("perched on the edge of randomness," as Toffler describes it) the couple with one child can come close to maximizing their autonomy.

Technology intrudes again, of course, whenever "autonomy" is speculated on: setting limits. Perhaps minimum fertility allows one to push back the limits, Neisuler suggests—but they are still there. The feeling is reflected often. If large families were never exactly indicative of faith in the future (because no one was seeing the future then), small ones are neither totally indicative of lack of faith. But we do see the future now, and there is a discernible caution. "We can't do much about the world we will bring our child into," explained a newly engaged student at East Carolina University. "Megasystems, bureaucracies, the fact that there is stockpiled around the world more than ten tons of TNT for every man, woman, and child alive—it's frightening. How can we know a child can grow up safely? At least by having only *one* we can maximize his chances for survival, for success."

"It works the other way, too, I assure you," Leona Train Rienow responded to the student, with what I can only call, or recall, as a serious smile. "Have one and you don't just give *him* a better chance for survival, you give everybody else more of a shot at survival, too." Certainly that's true, because one-child families, if predominant, would reduce human numbers. And perhaps it all gets back to human numbers. But that is not all that Ms. Rienow had in mind. A "functional only child" herself, who is married to an only child, she co-authored with her husband a landmark environmental treatise *Moment in the Sun* and has spearheaded several specific movements. She credits her environmental consciousness in part to the appreciation for privacy and space she developed during her ten years as an only child.

"The only child will be the child the future greatly

needs," she says, insisting, "Even if every awful thing we ever heard about the only child were true, we would *still* need to welcome and encourage single children, since an average of 'the only' is *our only* hope of bringing population into line with what our planet can sustain.

"But I mean more than that, more than just numbers. The only child will also be the kind of *citizen* the future needs. Think. Accustomed to space and privacy and freedom, will he tolerate assault by noise, pollution, crowding? I don't think so. He will involuntarily resist crowds and masses and love instead wild, open places—and, used to them, he will protect them. Heaven *help* us if we see instead a generation that can *adjust* to a teeming, dying world, with no wolves or whales or redwoods, no living oceans or wilderness or room for fantasy."

She trusts onlies to have "adjustment problems" in that one way at least, and hopes that in addition to being the doers and the thinkers they will also swell the ranks of rebels if our landscapes really start to darken. They just might do so. Many overrepresentations of only children among groups of distinguished people have been referred to. The one that matters to Lee Rienow is this: Of 112 individuals who hold key leadership positions with social reform and conservation groups, 34 are only children! That number is enough to more than hint that single children may be leaders in moral careers as well as professional ones.

Rienow's hypothesis begs (as long as we are being idealistic anyway) for a slight extension. The only child, we know, grows used to personal freedoms as well as personal space. Might he not be the first to anger if liberties were tampered with? Accustomed as he doubtless was to caring, reasoning, responsive parents, will he tolerate *un*reasoning, *un*responsive institutions?

Only children have no monopoly on righteous anger or defense of liberties of course! *Lots* of the *rest* of us are developing some rather nervous, guarded feelings about our privacy and space and freedom, too! But the mere chance or possibility that only children could develop such important attributes naturally and in excess *doesn't even have to be accepted* as any full or final "reason why" couples "should" consider having no more than a single child. Happily, these thoughts and possibilities for the future can merely supplement the other benefits that only children can bring to this generation of men and women now.

Appendix of
Questionnaires

I. QUESTIONNAIRE FOR ONLY CHILDREN

Circle T or F unless otherwise indicated. Also, feel free to add words to the T-F statements, write in margins, or otherwise personalize these pages. Questionnaires will be individually read, not machine scored.

1. I am very glad I am an only child.   T   F
2. I am generally glad I am an only child.   T   F
3. I often regret being an only child.   T   F
4. I sometimes regret being an only child.   T   F
5. I have no particular positive or negative feelings about my "onliness."   T   F
6. I have had no particular *awareness* of my "onliness."   T   F
7. Compared to others I know I feel I am: (write in "more" "less" or "equally")
   - _____ successful
   - _____ cooperative
   - _____ spoiled
   - _____ lonely
   - _____ intelligent
   - _____ accomplished
   - _____ relaxed about life in general
   - _____ satisfied with self
   - _____ satisfied with career achievement
   - _____ satisfied with social adjustment
   - _____ satisfied with sexual adjustment
   - _____ satisfied with total adjustment
8. I always wanted a (sister/brother). (Circle one *if* TRUE.)   T   F
9. I only recall wanting a sister or brother
   - in preschool years   T   F
   - in elementary school   T   F
   - in high school   T   F
   - college or after h.s.   T   F
   - as an adult   T   F
10. I never wanted a brother or sister.   T   F

11. I knew other only children when I was growing up.   T   F
12. I had a "fantasy" brother or sister or friend as a child.   T   F
13. I sometimes pretended a friend was my brother or sister.   T   F
14. I had many friends as a child.   T   F
15. I have many friends now.   T   F
16. I prefer a few close friends to a larger number of casual ones.   T   F
17. I have discussed with my parents their reasons for having only me.   T   F
18. If "True," please explain their reasons briefly.

19. If "False," why was this not discussed and what do you believe their reasons were?

20. Do you feel your parents benefited from having only you? If so, how?

21. What are advantages you feel *you* enjoyed as an (only) child? (If none, write "None.")

21a. As an adult?

22. List any disadvantages you feel you had or have. (If none, write "None.")

23. What *negative remarks* if any have you been subject to about your "onliness"? Please list—and explain circumstances briefly.

24. What are your responses to the above negative remarks?

25. My sex is _____ and my age is _____ .

26. My own preferred number of children to have would be _____ (0,1,2,3 or more) and the number of children I have now is _____ .

27. I believe prejudice against the only child is (circle one) slight —moderate—severe.

28. If there were an association for only children and families with a single child who face pressure to have another child, I would be interested.   T   F

29. In having or thinking about having a child or children I would be willing to adopt.   T   F

30. My parents are (circle one) married, divorced, separated, separated by death.

31. My parents' ages when they had me were _____ mother _____ father.

32. I live with my parents or one of them.   T   F

33. (If living separately) I visit my parent(s) often.   T   F

34. My parent(s) complain that I am inattentive.   T   F

35. I feel my parent(s) are too dependent on me
financially.   T   F

36. I feel my parent(s) are too dependent on me
emotionally.   T   F

37. I fear my parent(s)' emotional dependence on
me in later years.   T   F

38. I fear my parent(s)' financial dependence on me
in later years.   T   F

39. My job is (circle one) professional, secretarial,
clerical, mechanical, _____.
                                        (other)

40. My work is in the field of (circle one) transportation, education, arts, sciences, government, public service, factory,
social reform, _____.
                                        (other)

41. My devotion to my work is such that recreation
is minimal.   T   F

42. My co-workers are among my best friends.   T   F

43. Briefly describe your social or recreational life including:
favorite activities, number evenings out in a typical week,
whether you prefer large or small gatherings, etc.

44. If you have supported with time or money a community
theater, church group, museum, improvement association,
political organization, etc., please list.

45. My childhood hobbies included:

46. If you won honors in school such as prom queen, honor society, others, please list all you remember.

47. If you have won recognition in your work, please list awards, honors, other types of recognition

48. I am (circle one) single/ married/ separated/ divorced/ stable but nonmarital relationship.

48a. I am content with above status.   T   F

48b. If married, my spouse's birth order is (circle one) only/ eldest/ middle/ youngest.

49. I support the following ideas:

    women's liberation (major goals)   T   F
    reform of campaign financing   T   F
    guaranteed annual income   T   F
    gun control   T   F
    increased benefits for aged   T   F
    zero population growth   T   F
    strict environmental controls   T   F

50. Topics which this questionnaire failed to mention but which are relevant to the only child include:

OPTIONAL: *Please write your name and address if you are interested in receiving results of this questionnaire survey or other research on only children. Thank you.*

II. QUESTIONNAIRE FOR PARENTS OF ONLY CHILDREN

Circle T or F unless otherwise indicated. However, feel free to add words to the T-F statements, write in margins, or otherwise personalize this questionnaire. Responses *will* be individually read.

1. My having an only child was a deliberate decision.   T   F
2. I am very glad I have just one child.   T   F
3. I am generally glad I have just one child.   T   F
4. I often regret having just one child.   T   F
5. I sometimes regret having just one child.   T   F
6. Compared to other children of my child's peer group I feel my child is (write in "more" "less" "equally").

   _____ cooperative
   _____ successful in school
   _____ popular
   _____ spoiled
   _____ lonely
   _____ intelligent
   _____ creative and imaginative
   _____ happy

6a. A specific incident in which I have observed my child being (more, less, equally) *cooperative* in comparison to other children is: (please describe—perhaps a play situation).

7. My own birth order situation is _____ (only, eldest, middle, youngest) from a family of _____ children.
8. My spouse is _____ (only, eldest, etc.) from a family of ___ _____ children.
9. I have been criticized for having just one child.   T   F
10. My only child is a _____ (boy, girl) aged _____.

11. I believe my only child has been made aware of
    his or her "onliness."   T   F

12. I believe my child is happy to be an only child _____ (al-
    ways, generally, sometimes, never—other comment).

12a. My child has expressed a wish for a brother or sister _____
    __ (often, sometimes, never).

13. If my child expresses a wish for a sibling, I be-
    lieve this is partly due to attitudes of peers and
    their families.   T   F

14. Why, and *when*, did you decide to have only one child?
    (Please explain in as much detail as you wish.)

15. Have you definitely decided to have only one child?

16. If "No," on what factors will your decision rest? (economic,
    social criticism, others)

17. What advantages do *you* feel you have had . . . have now
    . . . and will have in the future as a result of having only
    one child?

18. What advantages do you feel your child has had and will
    have?

19. Please comment on any disadvantages you see for you or
    your child.

20. I believe social prejudice against one-child families to be: (circle one) (negligible, slight, moderate, serious, so severe as to jeopardize many individuals' decision to have only one child).

21. What criticisms have you received as the parent of an only child? (Please describe as many as you recall, and state circumstances briefly.)

22. What are your responses to the above criticisms?

23. Have you ever found yourself seeking out articles or books which would help justify your decision?

24. Do you feel that sufficient articles or books exist on the subject?

25. If you knew of a rap group in your town or city for parents of only children, would you attend?

26. If there were an association for parents of one child, would you be interested?

27. I support the following ideas:

women's liberation	T	F
reform of campaign financing	T	F
guaranteed annual income	T	F
gun control	T	F
zero population growth	T	F
increased benefits for aged	T	F
strict environmental controls	T	F

28. Do you feel your relationship with your spouse would improve, worsen, or remain the same if you had another child?

29. Do you feel your relationship with your child would improve, worsen, or remain the same if you had another child?

30. How do you feel other goals in your life (other than parenthood) would be affected by another increase in your family size?

31. My sex is _____. My age is _____. My marital status is (circle one): (single, married, separated, divorced, stable but nonmarital relationship).

32. Topics which I wish this questionnaire had brought up, but which it failed to bring up, include:

OPTIONAL: *Please write your name and address if you are interested in receiving results of this questionnaire survey or other research on only children.*

III. QUESTIONNAIRE FOR
THOSE PLANNING TO HAVE ONE CHILD

Please feel free to put answers on a separate paper—for more space—and use these questions as a guide only. You may have other comments and reactions you wish to make.

1. What has been your experience with only children—as children or adults? Consider in approaching this question: Did you know any only children when you were in school? envy them? Know many of them or only a few—or perhaps a few only children very well? Were you an only child and did you find it so satisfying you want to repeat the experience? What role does economics play in your perception of only children—they have more advantages, etc.

2. What are your reasons for planning to have an only child? Reasons of life-style? finance? ecology? What advantages do you feel you can give to a child if you have only one? What advantages do you feel you personally will have?

2a. Have you personally seen or heard of instances of serious sibling rivalry or simply lack of friendship among brothers and sisters?

3. Have you discussed with family, relatives, co-workers, neighbors, friends the fact that you will likely have only one child? What *reactions* have you encountered, and from whom? What have your responses been to these reactions?

4. If there were, in your area, an informal meeting or "rap group" among those who either have a single child, or plan a single child, would you be interested in attending such a group to share experiences and support? Whether or not you would be interested, do you feel there is a *need* for such groups?

IV. FAMILY COUNSELOR OPINION SURVEY:
SELECTED ASPECTS OF THE ONE-CHILD FAMILY

1. Would you comment on the idea that "the second child is easier"? To your observation, *is* the transition to the second child "easier" than the first? Why or why not?

2. Widespread disillusionment with parenthood has been noted. In general, are parents of one child happier than those who have more than one child?

3. Is the "empty nest" for parents of the only child less likely to represent a traumatic experience—less likely to prompt marital discord or separation?

Please sign your name and address:
Do you wish to receive summarized results of this and similar surveys?
Once more, sincere thanks.

V. PROFESSIONAL OPINION SURVEY ON THE ONLY CHILD

(Distributed to psychologists, sociologists, child psychiatrists)

Following is a partial list of outstanding artistic and creative personalities.

Hans Christian Anderson	Oscar Wilde
Charles Pierre Baudelaire	Ringo Starr
Antonia Brico	Burt Bacharach
Jean-Paul Sartre	Louise Lasser
Shirley Jones	John Simon
Hedy Lamarr	Kenneth Clark
Robert Louis Stevenson	Rex Reed
Anthony Newley	Leonardo da Vinci
Marilyn Monroe	Sammy Davis, Jr.
Lauren Bacall	Clark Gable
Elliott Gould	Betty Furness
Alexander Pope	Willy Brandt
Mary Astor	George Gamow (nuclear physicist)
Dick Cavett	William Randolph Hearst
Frank O'Connor	Charles Evans Hughes
Romain Gary	Franklin D. Roosevelt
Émile Zola	Eleanor Roosevelt

1. Might any impressions be ventured based on the fact that all of the above individuals are only children?

2. What factors influence the development of a creative imagination in childhood? Might an only child be favored in terms of these factors?

3. (a) On a scale of 1–10, how usual is rivalry among siblings: from rare (1) or nonexistent (0) to near-universal (9) or universal (10)?

   (b) On the same 1–10 scale, how usual is serious or destructive sibling rivalry?

   (c) Are feelings of "dethronement" or jealousy common on the part of an older child when a new sibling is brought into the family?

   (d) Regardless of childhood rivalry, do most *adult* sibling ties tend to be close? Or are superficial "obligatory" relationships more the rule than the exception? Please include one or more examples from your experience if possible.

(e) Please check one: I believe only children to be: _____ better adjusted in general than members of sibling groups; _____ in general, better adjusted or as well adjusted as members of sibling groups; _____ as well adjusted as members of sibling groups; _____ tending to be less well adjusted in general than individuals with siblings.

4. Are there advantages to being an only child? If so, what would the main advantage(s) seem to you to be?

4a. Are there disadvantages to being an only child? If so, what would the main disadvantage(s) seem to you to be?

5. What factors of social demography (urbanization, overpopulation, etc.) or human psychology (need for small groups in oversocialized world?) or other factors or any kind *might* forecast the one-child family as a principal or predominant family style of the future?

VI. DISTINGUISHED INDIVIDUAL SURVEY

(letter and reply card)

Dear Friend:

As part of my research on birth order, I would like to know how many individuals on a list of 3,000 distinguished men and women (gathered from *Who's Who* and other sources) are only children. Will you help me by returning the enclosed card?

Please remember when replying that the term "only child" is to some extent flexible. If, for example, you had a much younger or older brother or sister but essentially grew up alone, you should be counted as an only child.

Thank you very much. Your cooperation is appreciated.

Sincerely,

_____ I am an only child.

If not an only child, I am _____ (1st, 2nd, 3rd, etc.) of _____ __ children.

The number of children I presently have is _____ and the number I plan to have eventually is _____.

_____ I am interested in learning the results of this survey and any other current surveys relating to the only child.

_____

Signature (Optional)

References

INTRODUCTION

1. Linda J. Beckman, "Values of Parenthood Among Women Who Want an Only Child." Paper presented to American Psychological Association, Washington, D.C., September 3, 1976.

2. J.H. McCaghy and J.K. Skipper, "Strip-Teasers: The Anatomy and Career Contingency of a Deviant Occupation," *Social Problems*, Vol. 17 (1970), p. 301.

3. R.B. Goldblatt, *et al.*, "Birth Order, Personality Development, and Vocational Choice of Becoming a Carmelite Nun," *Journal of Psychology*, Vol. 85 (1973), p. 75.

4. Philip S. Very, "Relation Between Birth Order and Being a Beautician," *Journal of Applied Psychology*, Vol. 53, No. 2 (1969), pp. 149–51.

5. The basic research instrument created exclusively for this book was a series of questionnaires prepared for the following groups: only children, parents of only children, and couples who plan (firmly or tentatively) to have an only child. Responses for the first two of these three sample groups were checked against roughly equal numbers of control

group subjects (non-only children and parents of siblings) drawn from the same or similar sources: *i.e.,* recruited via notices in the same or similar professional, conservation, and alumni publications or newsletters. A second set of questionnaires was prepared and responses gathered from the following groups: psychologists belonging to the American Psychological Association; marriage and family counselors belonging to the American Association of Marriage and Family Counselors; members of the National Council on Family Relations; public school teachers; demographers and sociologists.

Finally, mailings to survey birth order of distinguished individuals were sent to representatives of the following groups: those listed in *Who's Who in America;* those representing the U.S. delegation at the 1976 Summer Olympic Games in Montreal; recipients of the National Institute of Arts and Letters awards in literature; women business leaders in the U.S. as identified by *Business Week* magazine; those holding positions of leadership with eleven national organizations concerned with social reform.

CHAPTER 1.

1. Failure to separate only and first-born children is common to many birth-order studies and surveys. Again and again one will read (as in Walter Toman's *Family Constellation*), "Aspiration levels, measured via numerical computation scores, were highest among *oldest siblings and single children.* . . . In responding to situations that required prediction of performance, *oldest siblings and single children* raised their estimates more often and by more and lowered them less often and by less, than did others. . . . Achievement motivation measured by T.A.T. stories was higher than average with *oldest siblings and single children.* . . ." Etc. While the two birth orders have some things in common (and it may well even be true that the secret of the first-born's success is that for a little while he or she was an only child), this still

seems insufficient reason for lumping the two together.

2. The concept of a "functional only child" as one separated by seven years or more from nearest sibling has been suggested by several students of the only child, notably Dr. Murray Kappelman. However, I think the wisest birth-order investigators are wary of such a short span of years. In fact, no matter what the span of years, is a second child often treated with the care and excitement of the first? In terms of certain other factors, however, thirteen years, as in this case of the astronauts, might almost be the same as those factors as experienced by an only child (notably: aloneness, autonomy). Except in rare cases, however, this book does not acknowledge the concept of a "functional only child."

3. Brian Sutton-Smith, J.M. Roberts, and B.C. Rosenberg, "The Dramatic Sibling," *Perceptual and Motor Skills,* Vol. 22 (1966), p. 993.

4. Walter and Eleonore Toman, "Sibling Positions of a Sample of Distinguished Persons," *Perceptual and Motor Skills,* Vol. 31 (1970), pp. 825–26.

5. Philip Allen, "Childhood Background of Success in a Profession," *American Sociological Review,* Vol. 20 (April 1955), pp. 186–90.

6. Donald R. Sweeney, *et al.,* "Note on Pain Reactivity and Family Size," *Perceptual and Motor Skills,* Vol. 31 (1970), p. 25.

7. Department of Health, Education, and Welfare, "A Review of the Actual and Expected Consequences of Family Size" (1974), p. 157.

8. John H. Dingle, *et al.,* "Illness in the Home: A Study of 25,000 Illnesses in a Group of Cleveland Families" (Cleveland: Case Western Reserve University Press, 1964).

9. John Nisbet, "Family Environment and Intelligence," *Eugenics Review,* Vol. 45 (1953), pp. 31–40.

10. J.W.B. Douglas, *The Home and the School* (London: Macgibbon and Kee, 1964).

11. Sukhendra Lal Chopra, "Family Size and Sibling Position as Related to Measured Intelligence," *Journal of Social Psychology,* Vol. 70 (1966), pp. 133–37.

12. E. J. Bradford, "Can Present Scholastic Standards Be Maintained?" *Journal of Education*, Vol. 3 (1925), pp. 186–98.
13. Thomas Kellaghan and John MacNamara, "Family Correlates of Verbal Reasoning," *Developmental Psychology*, Vol. 7 (1972), pp. 49–52.
14. I. Papavassiliou, "Intelligence and Family Size," *Population Studies*, Vol. 7 (1954), p. 222.
15. A. M. Lilienfield, *et al.*, "Mental Deficiency," *American Journal of Mental Deficiency*, Vol. 60 (1956), p. 557.
16. Lillian Belmont and Francis Marolla, "Birth Order, Family Size, and Intelligence," *Science*, Vol. 182 (1973), pp. 1096–1101.
17. C. Quensel, "The Interrelations of Marital Status, Fertility, Family Size and Intelligence Test Scores," *Population Studies*, Vol. 11 (1958), pp. 234–50.
18. Ruth B. Guilford and D. A. Worcester, "A Comparative Study of the Only and Non-Only Child," *Journal of Genetic Psychology*, Vol. 38 (1930), pp. 411–26.
19. Walter Toman, *Family Constellation* (New York: Springer, 1969), p. 246.
20. Bruno Bettelheim, *Truants from Life* (Glencoe, Illinois: Free Press, 1955).
21. Morris Rosenberg, "Society and the Adolescent Self-Image" (Princeton, New Jersey: Princeton University Press, 1965).
22. Daniel Goleman, "The Fertile Tension Between Discipline and Impulse," *Psychology Today* (October 1976), p. 53.

CHAPTER 2.

1. Erica Jong, *Fear of Flying* (New York: Holt, Rinehart & Winston, 1974).
2. Alfred Adler, *What Life Should Mean to You* (New York: Capricorn, 1958), p. 154.
3. Kathleen Norris, *Family Gathering* (Garden City, New York: Doubleday, 1959), p. 228.
4. Benjamin Spock, *Baby and Child Care* (New York: Pocket Books, 1970), 3rd edition, pp. 339–49.

References

5. Lucille Forer, *Birth Order and Life Roles* (Springfield, Illinois: Charles C. Thomas, 1969), p. 95.
6. Wyatt Cooper, *Families* (New York: Bantam), 1975.
7. Cooper, *Families*.
8. Cooper, *Families*.
9. Peter J. Ognibene, *Scoop: The Life and Politics of Henry M. Jackson* (New York: Stein and Day, 1975), p. 196.
10. Margaret Mead, *Redbook* (June 1974), p. 33.
11. Murray Kappelman, "The Only Child," *Glamour* (April 1975), p. 196.
12. C. Keith Connors, "Birth Order and Needs for Affiliation," *Journal of Personality*, Vol. 31 (1963), p. 408.
13. Stanley Schachter, *The Psychology of Affiliation* (Stanford, California: Stanford University Press, 1959).
14. Forer, *Birth Order and Life Roles*, p. 80.
15. Dorothy T. Dyer, "Are Only Children Different?" *Journal of Educational Psychology*, Vol. 36 (1945), p. 297.
16. Eda J. LeShan, "The Only Child." Pamphlet published by Public Affairs Committee of New York, 1971.
17. Merl E. Bonney, "Relationship Between Social Success and Family Size Among School Children Grades III to V," *Sociometry*, Vol. 7 (1944), p. 26.
18. R. B. Zajonc and G. Markus, "Birth Order and Intellectual Development," *Psychological Review*, Vol. 82 (1972), pp. 74–88.
19. The only exception has been a very brief paper by John Claudy of Palo Alto contending that only children tested at twelfth-grade level for certain IQ composites scored lower in ability than the average child from a two-child family. Claudy's sample, however, was smaller than any of the four major studies supporting the Zajonc theory.

CHAPTER 3.

1. Compared were: working mother of 1-year-old; working mother of 1- and 3-year-old; non-working mother of infant;

non-working mother of infant and 3-year-old; non-working mother of 8-year-old; non-working mother of 8- and 10-year-old; working mother of 7-year-old; working mother of 7- and 9-year-old; working mother of 5-year-old; working mother of 5- and 7-year-old; working mother of 12-year-old; working mother of 9- and 13-year-old.

2. Newsletter of the Institute for Social Research of the University of Michigan (Winter 1975).

3. Betty Rollin, *Today*, NBC, December 14, 1973.

4. Joyce Brothers, *Good Housekeeping* (July 1976).

5. William J. Lederer and Dr. Don D. Jackson, *The Mirages of Marriage* (New York: W. W. Norton, 1968), pp. 190–91.

6. Nadine Brozan, "The One-Child Family," *New York Times*, January 30, 1975.

7. W. G. Cobliner, "Some Maternal Attitudes Toward Conception," *Mental Hygiene*, Vol. 49 (1965), p. 555.

8. Judith Weinraub, "Behind School Success Is a Father Who Cares," *New York Times*.

9. Toni Falbo, "The Only Child as a Theoretical and Social Issue," unpublished, 1975.

10. Ivan Nye, *et al.*, "Family Size, Interaction, Affect, and Stress," *Journal of Marriage and the Family*, Vol. 32 (1970), p. 216.

CHAPTER 4.

1. Norman Fenton, "The Only Child," *Journal of Genetic Psychology*, Vol. 25 (1929), p. 547.

2. Department of Health, Education, and Welfare, "A Review of the Actual and Expected Consequences of Family Size" (1974), pp. 20–21.

3. Émile Zola, *Fécondité* (Paris: Fasquelle, 1899), p. 18.

4. One example is provided by a December 1927 issue of *Liberty* magazine. Brenda Ueland's article characterizes the only child as finicky and fearful and possessed of all the other traits we've heard so much of, and is accompanied by an illustration that is arresting: Seemingly enslaved parents bow

in homage to an only child who has an arrogant air and is seated on something much resembling a throne.

5. E. Wexberg, *Your Nervous Child* (New York: Boni Press, 1927), p. 178.

6. ———, "A Little Apology," *Ladies Home Journal* (November 1975).

7. Bernard Gould, "The Baby She Can Never Kiss," *Midnight* (May 3, 1976), p. 1.

8. This statement seems well grounded. For example, the over-representation of latter-borns in American and British populations of schizophrenics has been demonstrated consistently, the three major studies being Granville-Grossman, "Birth Order and Schizophrenia," *British Journal of Psychiatry,* Vol. 492 (1966), pp. 1119–126; Farina-Garmezy, "Birth Order of Recovered and Non-Recovered Schizophrenics," *Archives of General Psychiatry,* Vol. 9 (1963), pp. 224–28; Schooler, "Birth Order and Schizophrenia," *Archives of General Psychiatry,* Vol. 4 (1961), pp. 91–97.

   Several studies have also shown school-age only children to be underrepresented in delinquent populations.

9. Gideon Panter and Shirley Motter Linde, *Now That You've Had Your Baby* (New York: McKay, 1976), p. 197.

10. The importance of this paper, "Birth Order and Intelligence," lies in the number of times it has been cited in other sources. Several secondary sources quote Nichols, the author, as though he separated onlies from first-borns, but the paper itself does not do so.

11. The Gallup questionnaire asked only that respondents "Check box which indicates age of your children who now live at home," followed by age categories. It would have been terribly easy to ask, "How many children do you have?" but as it is, a respondent may have checked box 0–5 with *no way* to tell *how many* children under age 5 she has.

12. Jacob Arlow, "The Only Child," *Psychoanalytic Quarterly* (1972), p. 507.

CHAPTER 5.

1. Sammy Davis, Jr., *Yes, I Can* (New York: Farrar, Straus & Giroux, 1965).

CHAPTER 6.

1. Erwin S. Solomon, *et al.,* "Social and Psychological Factors Affecting Fertility," *Milbank Memorial Fund Quarterly,* Vol. 39 (1956), pp. 160–77.

CHAPTER 7.

1. P. G. Zimbardo of Stanford University has conducted a number of field studies on aggression and vandalism as they relate to crowding. In one interesting experiment, cars were left abandoned on the streets of a large city and a small city. The car in the large city was attacked almost immediately, and completely wrecked within two days. The car left unprotected on a street in the small city remained untouched for more than a week, at which point its weary observers ended the experiment and drove it away.
2. S. Stansfeld Sargent and Kenneth R. Stafford (eds.), *Basic Teachings of the Great Psychologists* (New York: Dolphin, 1965), p. 229.
3. Alvin Toffler, *The Eco-Spasm Report* (New York: Bantam, 1975), pp. 55–64.
4. Anne H. Ehrlich and Paul R. Ehrlich, *Population/Resources/ Environment* (San Francisco: W.H. Freeman Co., 1970), p. 190.

Index

Index